LITTLE STITCHES

100+ Sweet Embroidery Designs • 12 Projects

Aneela Hoey

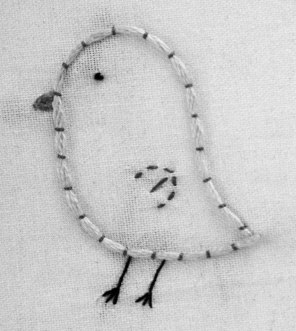

stashBOOKS®

an imprint of C&T Publishing

Dedication

This book is dedicated to Asha and Ciara; thank you for putting all these playful ideas in my head. This book would not exist without you—xoxo.

Acknowledgments

Thank you to all my blog readers, who have given me the support I needed to push my creative ideas.

Thank you to Cheryl Freydberg at Moda Fabrics for giving me the chance to design fabric for such a unique and wonderful company; to my husband, P. J., who doesn't know what to make of all this but goes along with it anyway; and to my friend Zoe Harper for making light work of any crisis.

Thank you also to Susanne Woods at Stash Books for this amazing opportunity and to Cynthia Bix for making all my words sound like I know what I'm talking about.

Text and Artwork copyright © 2012 by Aneela Hoey

Photography copyright © 2012 by C&T Publishing, Inc.

Publisher: Amy Marson

Creative Director: Gailen Runge

Art Director / Book Designer:
Kristy K. Zacharias

Editor: Cynthia Bix

Technical Editors: Janice Wray
and Gailen Runge

Production Coordinator: Zinnia Heinzmann

Production Editor: Alice Mace Nakanishi

Illustrator: Aneela Hoey

Photo Assistant: Cara Pardo

Photography by Christina Carty-Francis
and Diane Pedersen of C&T Publishing, Inc.,
unless otherwise noted

Published by Stash Books, an imprint of C&T Publishing, Inc., P.O. Box 1456,
Lafayette, CA 94549

Library of Congress Cataloging-in-Publication Data

Hoey, Aneela, 1971-

  Little stitches : 100+ sweet embroidery designs - 12 projects / Aneela Hoey.

    pages cm

  ISBN 978-1-60705-525-9

  1. Embroidery--Patterns. I. Title.

  TT771.H64 2012

  746.44--dc23

                              2012004060

Printed in China

10 9 8 7 6 5 4 3 2 1

CONTENTS

INTRODUCTION

I have always loved to make things—from the paper clothes I made for my paper dolls, to curtains and quilts, to jam, and even to plants, which I like to propagate. If you can make it, I'll certainly try it.

Embroidery was something I learned to do in school during needlework class, when I was eight years old. I still have the drawstring bag, stitched with the My Little Pony motif, that I completed at age sixteen for the practical part of my CSE (United Kingdom Certificate of Secondary Education) Needlework Exam. Somehow, that bag hasn't fallen apart in the slightest, despite almost 25 years of constant use.

I thought I had long forgotten the skills I learned in those early years. But when I was asked to take part in an online embroidery swap a few years ago, there were those old skills, waiting for me to put them to use again. This time around, I have become particularly enamored with both making embroidery and creating patterns for stitching. I love the creative outlet embroidery provides, as well as its therapeutic properties. (I put most of my days "to bed" with a few stitches and a cup of chamomile tea.)

In this book, I offer basic instructions for simple stitches, along with a generous selection of original embroidery patterns, which are also printed on transfer paper so you can easily iron them onto your fabric and stitch away. I've also included twelve projects—from sewing accessories like a pincushion and needle case to whimsical but practical items like a hot water bottle cover—that you can embroider and sew.

Many of my pieces are very playful in nature, because that's how I feel when I'm stitching. Both the subjects I stitch and the stitches I use are happy and creative—part of my grown-up playtime. I hope this book helps you find some fun playtime too.

EMBROIDERY BASICS

Whether you are an accomplished stitcher or a complete beginner, a little time spent going over the basics will be well worth your while before you start on the projects in this book.

Embroidery Tool Kit

One of the best things about deciding to try your hand at embroidery is that it is very low in cost to undertake. Only a handful of tools are needed, and these tools are both widely available and easy to obtain. The following is a breakdown of the tools you will need.

EMBROIDERY HOOP

Hoops are measured by their diameter. Both wooden and plastic versions are available; what you decide to use is purely a matter of personal preference and what is readily available to you. I have always used wooden hoops, although I do like the pretty look of plastic ones. For best results, choose a hoop size large enough to accommodate your embroidery image. To make the smaller projects in this book, like the *Empire State Building Needle Case* (page 42), you will need a 5″ (13cm) hoop. Medium-sized projects vary; some, such as the *Christmas Wrapping Stocking* (page 88), require a 7″ (18cm) hoop, and others, such as the *Row, Row Your Boat Patchwork Cushion Cover* (page 72), require an 8″ (20cm) hoop. You will

need a 10″ (25cm) hoop to make large projects, such as the *Let's Go Fly a Kite Baby Quilt* (page 78). Check the project you wish to make for required hoop sizes.

To tighten up your embroidery hoop, keep a small screwdriver close at hand.

FABRIC

I always stitch on good-quality 100% cotton fabric. I think if you are going to spend time and effort making something that you will want to keep for a very long time, you want it to stay looking its best. For this reason, I never use synthetic fabrics. White cotton fabric is my preferred choice; you may also wish to consider off-white and solid-colored cottons or prewashed linen.

EMBROIDERY PATTERNS

All the embroidery patterns for the projects offered here can be found at the back of the book, printed on both regular paper (pages 136–151) and iron-on transfer paper (pullout pages P1 and P2). You'll find the

project patterns and three alternative patterns for each project, as well as a nicely sized haul of additional patterns for you to try. If you wish to substitute one of the additional patterns in a sewing project, choose one similar in size to the suggested options in the project pages. No stitching suggestions are provided for the additional patterns, so if you are new to embroidery, it is best to start with the patterns that have instructions in the project pages.

The transfers are printed with heat-transferable ink; transfers can usually be used more than once. Keep any used transfers in an envelope for a future project.

EMBROIDERY FLOSS

I always use six-stranded cotton embroidery floss, which is widely available in a variety of deliciously colored hues and which is inexpensive to buy. As the name suggests, the strands, or plies, can be separated so you can use from one to six of them. The number of strands you choose to use can give either delicacy or weight to the various elements in your design, thereby creating textural interest and depth.

Separating the Strands

Cut a length of around 15″ of floss from the skein. Hold the floss in one hand and gently pull out the number of strands you wish to use. Do not pull too hard, or the threads will become tangled up and knotted.

Storing Flosses

Many stitchers like to wind their flosses onto small cards and store them neatly in boxes. Personally, I find this tedious and would much rather be stitching instead of winding! I keep all my floss skeins in a see-through plastic zip pouch that is about 12″ × 6″. You can find this kind of pouch in stationery shops or even drugstores. I gather all the cut and unused strands of floss into a loose ball (like a floss "tumbleweed"), and store them in the corner of the pouch. An advantage of storing floss in this way is that it's very easy to throw the pouch into my bag for stitching on the go.

Floss separates into 6 strands.

NEEDLES

It is fine to use ordinary sewing needles for your embroidery designs. However, it's worth seeking out embroidery needles; these have a longer eye, which makes it a lot easier to thread up to six strands of floss through at once. These needles glide through the fabric a whole lot easier too, which is particularly useful when making filling stitches in embroidery. Embroidery needles are inexpensive and widely available.

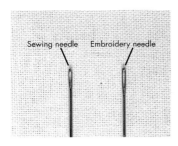

Sewing needle   Embroidery needle

SCISSORS

To cut embroidery floss easily and neatly, use very sharp scissors. Embroidery scissors or small regular sewing scissors with sharp, pointed blades are the best kinds to use.

PREPARE THE FABRIC

For most of the projects in this book, the embroidery pattern is applied to the center of the fabric that you will be stitching on. Preparing the fabric will help you center the pattern evenly. First, press the fabric smooth with an iron. Then, fold it in half across the width and crease it with the palm of your hand all along the fold. Now, fold it in half lengthwise and crease again in the same way. These creases will create guide marks to help you position the transfer in the center of the fabric (or off-center, if required).

Note: For a few projects in this book, the pattern is placed off-center; please refer to the individual project instructions for placement guidance.

Each pattern is offered in both an iron-on transfer option and a printed pattern option. Transfer the design, using the instructions for your chosen method (below and page 12).

APPLY THE IRON-ON TRANSFER

To use the iron-on transfer patterns in this book (pullout pages P1 and P2), cut out your chosen pattern using paper scissors, making sure to leave a minimum of ¼″ of extra space all around it. Use a dry iron set on high heat, though not so hot that it will create scorch marks on the fabric. With the fabric right side up, heat the fabric for 4–5 seconds. Place the transfer (wrong side up) in position. Press for 12–15 seconds. (Note: Do not glide the iron across the fabric, because this can cause the image to blur.) Carefully lift off the iron. Holding the transfer in position at one side, carefully lift up the opposite corner to see if the image has transferred successfully. If not, carefully lower the transfer and press for a few more seconds. The transfers can be used several times but will grown fainter with each use. The transferred ink will fade with washing but will not entirely disappear. Plan to cover the lines with your stitches. If the possibility of lines showing is a concern for you, use one of the methods described in Transfer the Printed Patterns (page 12).

TRANSFER THE PRINTED PATTERNS

To use the printed patterns in this book (pages 136–151), trace or photocopy your chosen pattern onto a piece of thin paper. Place the copied pattern right side up on a table and tape it in place. Position the fabric on top, right side up. Lightly trace the pattern onto your fabric using a soft pencil or a soluble or disappearing ink fabric marker. If it is difficult to see through your fabric, it might help to use a lightbox or hold the fabric up to a window.

Alternatively, you can use an iron-on transfer pencil or photocopy the design onto a fusible wash-away product such as Wash-Away Stitch Stabilizer (by C&T Publishing). Always refer to the manufacturer's instructions to use the product. Please be aware that some transfer methods will produce a design the reverse of that shown in my projects. Your project will be just as nice either way. However, be aware of designs that have words in them, or other designs such as a book that opens right to left, to be sure your transfer method does not reverse the design. Also, if your design is reversed, some embroidery references in the instructions may then be reversed. Always refer to the project photo for clarification.

FIX THE FABRIC IN THE HOOP

Separate the two rings of the hoop, place the smaller ring in front of you on a flat surface, lay your fabric on top, right side up, and place the larger ring over the fabric. Gently adjust into place so that the smaller bottom ring fits neatly inside the larger ring. Carefully tighten the screw top a little. Holding the hoop steady with one hand, use the other to gently pull the loose fabric outside of the hoop, all around the edge, to smooth the fabric in the hoop. Using a screwdriver, tighten the screw top a little more, gently pull the fabric all around a little more, and tighten again with the screwdriver. Continue like this until the fabric is smooth and taut but not stretched. You are now ready to start stitching.

Embroidery Stitches

In this section, you will find instructions for the eleven basic stitches needed to make the embroideries in this book. These are all very simple, easy-to-learn stitches. As you read through the instructions, I strongly suggest that you do so with a threaded needle and fabric in hand (the fabric does not need to be hooped). The stitch instructions will make much more sense if you practice the stitches. Spending a little time getting your stitches even and straight will allow you to approach the actual patterns with more confidence.

OUTLINE AND FILLING STITCHES

Sometimes a stitch is used only to outline an area. For example, the boy's sweater in the embroidery shown (below) is outlined using Split Stitch (page 15). Sometimes the outlined area is then filled (usually in the same stitch as the outline); the boy's trousers are outlined and filled using Backstitch (page 14), and his hair is outlined and filled using Split Stitch (page 15). For more about outlining and filling, see How to Use the Stitches (page 23).

Detail from Row, Row Your Boat Patchwork Cushion Cover
(full project on page 72)

STARTING AND FINISHING STITCHES

Take the 15″ length of floss that you separated into strands (refer to Separating the Strands, page 10), and thread your needle with the required number of strands. Make a small knot at the end of the longest tail of floss.

Make your stitches of choice. To finish, take your floss to the back of the embroidery and make a small knot close to the back. Cut off any excess floss, leaving a small tail about ½″ long.

TIP

When embroidering with only one or two strands of floss, you will need to make a larger knot to anchor the thinner threads firmly.

BACKSTITCH

USES: OUTLINE AND FILLING

Backstitch is my most-used stitch! You could complete any of the patterns in this book just by using this stitch on its own and to great effect. It is very plain in character but adds a lovely contrast when used with more frilly or showy stitches. Backstitch also makes a great outline stitch, as in *Bicycle Girl,* where the stitch outlines the face, neck, and legs, as well as the wheel spokes. It also works very well when used as a double outline, and it's a great filler, as shown in Filling in Rows (page 23).

For best results, keep your stitches as straight and as evenly sized as possible. The first stitch is always made forward; all subsequent stitches are made backward. The finished look of Backstitch is of a continuous line of stitching with no gaps in between.

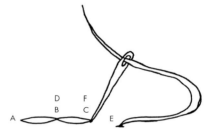

1. Bring the needle to the front of the fabric (A). Make a short stitch about ⅛″ long (B).

2. Bring the needle back out to the front of the fabric, about ⅛″ away from where the previous stitch ended (C).

3. Reinsert the needle at the same point at which the previous stitch ended (D).

4. Repeat Steps 2 and 3 until you have finished stitching the required element (E, F).

Bicycle Girl *(page 60)*

SPLIT STITCH

USES: OUTLINE AND FILLING

The very useful Split Stitch has a beautifully decorative finish. This stitch works well as an outline—shown on the small chick in *Big Chick, Little Chicks*—and as a double outline. You can use it to replicate a chain or a braid. As a filling stitch, it can be used in many ways. You can use it in rows, as described in Filling in Rows (page 23), or apply it in special ways to create a knitted fabric look, as described in Techniques for Special Effects (page 27).

This stitch is made similar to Backstitch, with a slight difference at the end. As with Backstitch, the first stitch is always made forward, and all subsequent stitches are made backward.

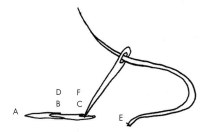

1. Bring the needle to the front of the fabric (A). Make a short stitch about ⅛″ long (B).

2. Bring the needle back out to the front of the fabric, about ⅛″ away from where the previous stitch ended (C).

3. Reinsert the needle just inside the previous stitch, between the strands of floss (D). This will split the previous stitch, hence the name.

4. Repeat Steps 2 and 3 until you have finished stitching the required element (E, F).

Detail from Big Chick, Little Chicks *(page 61)*

FRENCH KNOT

Basically, French Knot is a decorative knot that sits on the fabric's surface. It creates a lovely raised bobble-like contrast to other stitches. Use it to create a cherry, the knot in a hair ribbon, or a small flower head as in *Lily of the Valley*, among other things. French Knots work well on their own or collectively as a filling stitch, as shown in Allover Filling (page 26).

Detail from Lily of the Valley *(page 118)*

You can vary the size of the knot either by changing the number of times you wrap the thread around the needle or by changing the number of strands of floss you use.

1. Bring the needle through to the front of the work. As close to the entry point as possible, reenter and then exit the fabric with the tip of the needle, about ⅛" apart, picking up a few threads of the fabric—but don't pull the needle through. (Figure A)

2. Wrap the floss, fairly tightly, 3 times around the front half of the needle. (Figure B)

3. Holding down the wrapped threads with the thumb of your nonsewing hand, grab the front part of the needle with the thumb and forefinger of your opposite hand. Gently pull the needle and thread through the wrapped thread. This should make a nice, neat knot close to the fabric.

4. Insert the needle behind the knot and pull the remaining thread through to the back of the fabric. Continue making more French Knots, or tie off the floss on the back of the fabric if you are done. (Figure C)

To use French Knot as a filling stitch, first outline the area to be filled with Backstitch (this gives a nice neat edge to the area). Work French Knots, either close together or evenly spaced, to fill the outlined area.

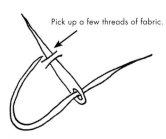

Pick up a few threads of fabric.

Figure A

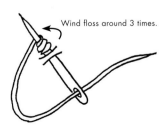

Wind floss around 3 times.

Figure B

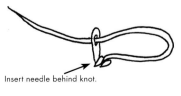

Insert needle behind knot.

Figure C

COUCHING STITCH

USES: **OUTLINE AND FILLING**

Couching Stitch is made using two separate threads, usually in contrasting colors and thicknesses, to create a beautifully intricate-looking stitch. It's very useful for depicting woven fabric and baskets. Use it as an outline stitch, as in *An Apple a Day,* or as a filling stitch, as shown in Filling in Rows (page 23), to neatly fill the area.

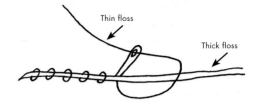

An Apple a Day *(page 118)*

1. Select 2 flosses—one thick (such as 6 strands in beige) and the other thin (such as 1 strand of turquoise). Thread the needle with the thicker thread and bring it through to the front of the fabric. Lay the thread over the pattern line you wish to make. This can be a curved or straight line. Remove the needle from the thread, if desired.

2. Thread another needle with the thinner thread and bring it through to the front of the fabric. Use this thread to make small stitches over the thicker thread at intervals.

To use Couching Stitch for filling, outline first in Couching Stitch, then work rows of the same stitch as described in Filling in Rows (page 23).

TIP

In this book, all instructions for Couching Stitch are given as follows: "Pink/Red, 6/1." This means that you would use six strands of pink floss as the thick thread and one strand of red thread as the thin thread.

STRAIGHT STITCH

USES: SINGLE STITCH

Straight Stitch is simply a single stitch. It is most commonly used on its own—as in *Christmas Wrapping Stocking,* to create an eye, for example. Straight Stitches can also be grouped together in an ordered form, as for the hedgehog spikes in *Little Hedgehog* (page 41), or in random scattered form, like the blades of grass in *Little Deer* (page 128).

Detail from Christmas Wrapping Stocking *(full project on page 88)*

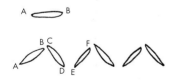

1. For a single stitch, bring the needle to the front of the fabric (A); then exit the fabric 1 stitch length away (B).

2. For grouped stitches, simply repeat the stitch at whatever angle is needed for the design (C–F).

CROSS-STITCH

USES: DECORATIVE

Cross-Stitch is made up of two straight stitches taken diagonally, one on top of the other, to make an X. It is most commonly used when making counted cross-stitch embroideries made up entirely of Cross-Stitches. The patterns in this book primarily feature individual Cross-Stitches to create charming decorative effects, as in *Bird in a Hoop.*

Detail from Bird in a Hoop *(page 114)*

1. Bring the needle to the front of the fabric. From the top left (A), make a diagonal stitch to the bottom right (B).

2. Bring the needle to the front of the fabric at (C) and make a second stitch, overlapping the first, from the top right to the bottom left (D).

RUNNING STITCH

USES: OUTLINE AND FILLING

A row of Straight Stitches in a line is known as Running Stitch. The finished look of Running Stitch is a very open stitch that contrasts well with other stitches. Use it as either an outline, as in *Puppy Dog Tails,* or a filling stitch, as described in Filling in Rows (page 23). A more decorative variation of Running Stitch can be created by alternating long and short stitches.

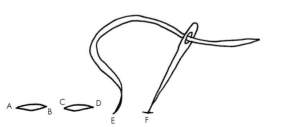

Puppy Dog Tails *(page 41)*

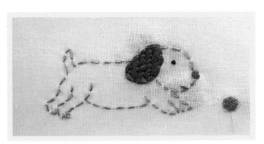

1. With needle and thread at the front of the fabric (A), take a small stitch about ⅛″ long (B).

2. Bring the needle up to the front about ⅛″ (or 1 stitch length) away from the last stitch (C).

3. Continue the line of stitching by repeating Steps 1 and 2 (D, E, F).

SEED STITCH

USES: FILLING

Seed Stitch is a filling stitch (see Allover Filling, page 26) made up of scattered Straight Stitches that are all the same length and usually stitched in random directions, as shown in the area at the rounded end of *Popsicle*. It looks great when outlined in Backstitch using a different number of threads, in either the same or a different color of floss.

Detail from *Popsicle (page 103)*

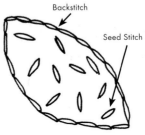

1. Begin by outlining the area to be filled using Backstitch (page 14).

2. To fill, work from one edge. Bring the needle to the front of the fabric and make a Straight Stitch (page 18).

3. Continue making evenly spaced and evenly sized Straight Stitches in a scattered formation to fill the entire area.

SCATTER STITCH

USES: FILLING

Scatter Stitch is a less usual way to use Straight Stitch (page 18) as a filling stitch. This stitch comprises Straight Stitches of different lengths, stitched close together and haphazardly scattered. Scatter Stitch is very useful in creating the look of a much-loved and well-worn toy, like the horse toy in *My Favorite Hobby Horse Cushion Cover,* or when re-creating the look of animal fur. Scatter Stitch filling can be outlined effectively with either more Scatter Stitch or Backstitch.

1. Begin by outlining the area to be filled using Backstitch, or first work Scatter Stitch around the area as described below. Then fill in the rest of the area.

2. Bring the needle to the front of the fabric and make a Straight Stitch of any length.

3. Bring the needle back out to the front and make another Straight Stitch of a different length and at a different angle to the first.

4. Continue making further stitches in the same way, filling any gaps as you go.

Scatter Stitches placed randomly and close together.

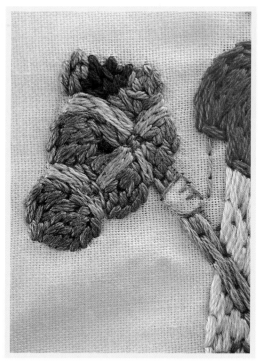

Detail from My Favorite Hobby Horse Cushion Cover *(full project on page 64)*

CHAIN STITCH

USES: OUTLINE AND FILLING

Chain Stitch is a decorative stitch composed of linked "chains"—perfect for effects like the swing ropes in *Cherry on the Tree Swing*. You can also use it as textured filler, as described in Filling in Rows (page 23). This stitch is similar in appearance to Split Stitch (page 15) but is worked differently.

Detail from Cherry on the Tree Swing *(page 85)*

1. Bring the needle to the front of the fabric (A).

2. On the fabric surface, form a loop with the first inch or so of floss. Hold this loop in place with the thumb of your nonsewing hand. Pass the needle to the back of the embroidery at the same point where you came up (B), and then bring it back out to the front again, about ⅛″ away and inside the loop (C). Pull the needle and floss gently to tighten the loop into a link.

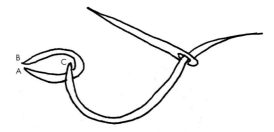

3. Repeat Step 2 to make the number of links needed.

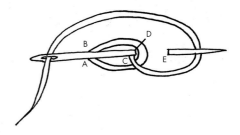

SATIN STITCH

Satin Stitch is used as a filling stitch as described in Filling in Rows (page 23). This stitch is made up of closely worked, parallel straight stitches, most usually at a slight angle, as shown in the scooter surface in *Scoot*. The overall surface texture of the finished stitches appears smooth and glossy, like satin.

Detail from Scoot *(page 86)*

1. Bring the needle to the front of the fabric at one side of the shape to be filled (A).

2. Work a Straight Stitch (page 18) on a slight angle, extending across the shape to the opposite side (B).

3. Bring the needle back out to the front of the embroidery, right next to the first stitch on the first side (C), and work a second stitch parallel to the first. Exit to the back of the embroidery on the opposite side (D).

For best results, work the stitches close together and keep the angle consistent.

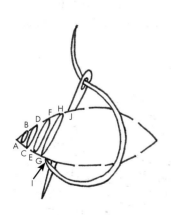

How to Use the Stitches

In this book, stitches are worked in one of two ways—as outline stitches or as filling stitches.

OUTLINE STITCHES

Stitches suitable for outlining include the following:

Backstitch · Split Stitch
Couching Stitch · Running Stitch
Chain Stitch

To work a stitch as an outline, simply follow the pattern lines using the directions for the individual stitch. To create a bolder effect, you can use these stitches to make a double outline. A double outline contrasts nicely with single outlines as well as with loosely filled areas, as shown with the double Backstitch outline in *Little Robin*.

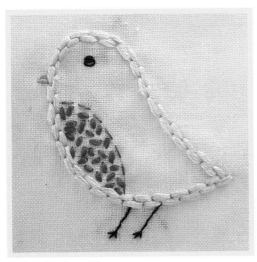

Little Robin (*page 95*)

FILLING STITCHES

Filling stitches are a big part of the look of the embroideries shown in this book. Filling techniques are very easy once you know how, so spend a little time practicing them. Grab a piece of fabric and a threaded needle, and let's go over the basics.

Filling in Rows

Stitches suitable for filling in rows include the following:

Backstitch · Split Stitch
Couching Stitch · Running Stitch
Chain Stitch · Satin Stitch

In these instructions, we'll use Backstitch. The charm of filling in this way is the lovely offset look it creates.

London Bus (*page 53*) with filled-in rows of Backstitch

1. Outline the area to be filled.

2. Using the same stitch (in this case Backstitch) and beginning in the top left corner of the area to be filled, start making a vertical row of stitching parallel to the left-hand outline. This row is worked top to bottom.

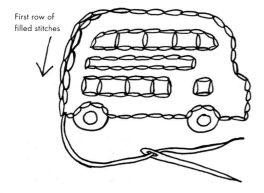

First row of filled stitches

Filled Backstitch detail from London Bus *(page 53)*

3. When you get to the bottom of this first filled row, start making a second vertical row, this time working from the bottom to the top. To create an offset effect, begin each stitch at the midway point of the stitch to the left of it. End the stitch at the midway point of the next stitch in the previous row.

4. Work the third row top to bottom and so on. Continue until the whole area has been filled.

The method for filling in rows is the same whether you are working in Backstitch, Split Stitch, Running Stitch, Chain Stitch, or Couching Stitch or whether you are working in vertical, horizontal, or even curved rows. Filling in with Satin Stitch, as in *Scoot* (page 86), differs from the other stitches in that each row is made of a single stitch and it isn't usually outlined.

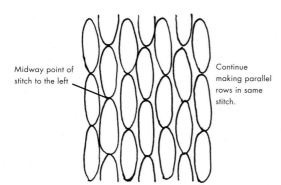

Midway point of stitch to the left

Continue making parallel rows in same stitch.

A Sweet Fox *(page 129)*
with filled-in Split Stitch.

Detail from "Oh, My Balloon"
Hot Water Bottle Cover
(full project on page 120),
with Backstitch filling worked
in curved rows

Detail from
Singing Cherry Tree
(page 109), showing
trunk with filled-in
Running Stitch

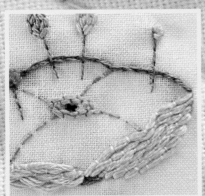

Detail from
Notions *(page 129),*
showing pincushion
with filling of
Couching Stitch

Allover Filling

Some stitches suit filling an area in a scattered, or "allover," formation rather than in rows. Stitches to work in this way include the following:

Scatter Stitch · Seed Stitch · French Knot

You can make the stitches close together or spaced apart. For instructions on how to fill using these stitches, refer to the individual stitch descriptions in Embroidery Stitches (page 13).

Detail of Cherry *(page 101), showing fruit filled in with Seed Stitch*

Detail of My Favorite Hobby Horse Cushion Cover *(full project on page 64), showing horse's head filled in with Scatter Stitch*

Hoot the Owl *(page 59), showing owl wings filled in with French Knots*

Techniques for Special Effects

Once you have gotten the hang of the stitches, you can learn how to use them in special ways to create visual interest in your embroidered pieces. There are several easy ways to do this.

VARY THE NUMBER OF FLOSS STRANDS

Varying the number of floss strands is a great way to create a sense of depth in a design. Elements that are worked in four to six strands of floss will "move forward" and attract the eye. This is a very useful way of highlighting the main subject in an embroidery—a dress or other garment on a figure, for example. Areas worked in one or two strands, on the other hand, will draw less attention and can work well for background elements. For example, a tree worked with fewer strands can add structure and location to an embroidered piece, without overshadowing the main subject.

Use varying numbers of strands to give distinctive characteristics to elements in a design. When replicating the delicacy necessary in facial features or in the sheerness of silk, for example, using one strand of floss will create the right effect. When creating a more solid object, such as a basket or an object made of wood, using four or more strands will convey a sense of bulk and sturdiness.

In *Nutty the Squirrel,* the main body part is made using six strands of floss, so it appears sturdy and more in focus, while the tail is made using one strand, which makes it softer, in keeping with its bushy quality. Playing with the number of strands you use in your design will help make a seemingly simple design more believable as a sum of its many textured parts.

Nutty the Squirrel *(page 69)*

COMBINE OUTLINE AND FILLING STITCHES

As with varying the number of floss strands, combining stitches can create visual interest and clarity. Use six strands of floss in a filled stitch to embroider the elements you most want to highlight in a design. Use one strand of floss as an outline to embroider the parts of the design that need to be the least noticeable.

In *Little Red Riding Hood,* the cape and bow are outlined and filled using six strands of floss, making them catch the eye and play a more prominent part in the finished piece. Meanwhile, the dress, legs, and face are made using fewer floss strands and are outlined only, making them less noticeable and more delicate.

USE STITCHES TO REPLICATE DIFFERENT MATERIALS

Certain stitches lend themselves particularly well to re-creating the look and feel of a particular material or object. Choosing the right stitch for the right element will make a design look instantly more realistic and interesting. For example, use French Knots (page 16) to resemble juicy, fat cherries, as in *Cherry on the Tree Swing,* or use a Couching Stitch (page 17) to create the look of a woven basket.

Detail from Cherry on the Tree Swing *(page 85)*

Little Red Riding Hood *(page 84)*

SPECIAL TECHNIQUES

Following are a couple of special situations that call for unusual stitching techniques.

Striped Knitted Scarf

Detail from A Washing Day Zip Pouch
(full project on page 54)

I used a special Split Stitch technique in the embroidery patterns for both *A Washing Day Zip Pouch* (page 54) and *Scoot* (page 86) in order to replicate the look of a striped, knitted scarf. Here is the method, illustrated using the scarf from the pattern for *A Washing Day Zip Pouch.*

1. Thread the needle with red floss (Color 1). Working from left to right, make a horizontal row of vertical Straight Stitches.

2. Working from right to left, start a second row of stitches beneath the first; make a vertical stitch beginning about ⅛″ below the stitch immediately above it and ending just inside the stitch above (splitting the stitch). Continue across, making the horizontal row of Split Stitches in this way. After the last stitch in the row is complete, leave the floss at the back of your work.

3. Unthread the needle to use for the next color (or use a new needle for Color 2). Thread the needle with aqua floss (Color 2). Working from left to right, make a horizontal row of Split Stitches as in Step 2. Make another row, working from right to left. Leave the floss at the back of your work after the last stitch.

4. Repeat Step 3, alternating colors down the length of the scarf.

Note: In the *Scoot* pattern (page 86), the rows are worked in exactly the same way, but making vertical rows of horizontal stitches with only one row in each color.

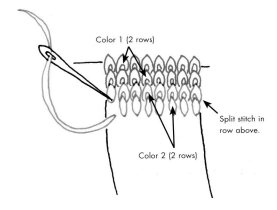

Color 1 (2 rows)

Split stitch in row above.

Color 2 (2 rows)

Decorative Stitches over Embroidered Stitches

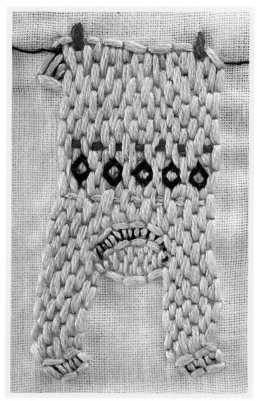

Detail from A Washing Day Zip Pouch
(full project on page 54)

In several embroideries in this book, such as *A Washing Day Zip Pouch* (page 54), *My Favorite Hobby Horse Cushion Cover* (page 64), and *Scoot* (page 86), decorative stitches are made on top of already-embroidered areas. This means that there are no pattern lines to follow when making these decorative stitches. Following is the method I use to help keep these stitches

neat and even, illustrated using the sweater from the pattern for *A Washing Day Zip Pouch*.

1. Outline and fill in the main shape (in this case, the sweater).

2. Carefully, so as not to snag any stitches, place sewing pins into the embroidery to mark the top and bottom positions of the decorative stitches to be made. Refer to the pictures of the finished embroidery to help guide you in placing the pins.

3. Using the decorative stitch pattern and the picture of the finished embroidery on the project pages for reference, embroider the decorative stitch pattern onto the embroidered area (sweater). Make each stitch in the usual way, taking it through to the back of the work after each stitch is made. If you find it difficult to embroider these stitches, try switching to a sharper/finer needle or to an embroidery needle. Go carefully, gently wiggling the needle through so as not to snag or pull the previously made stitches.

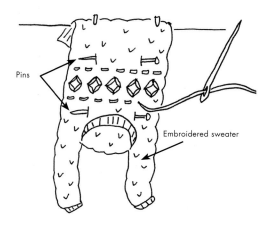

Pins

Embroidered sweater

MAKE FACES AND BODIES

Detail from My Favorite Hobby Horse Cushion Cover
(full project on page 64)

When I first began embroidering, the parts of the design I feared making the most were the faces, arms, and legs. It's essential to get these right in order to make the embroidery look believable. Many of my embroideries feature children, and a child's face must embody the delicate characteristics necessary to make it appear young and childlike. Through trial and error, I have developed a series of guidelines that I follow to enable me to make this process far, far less scary! This is how I do it.

- Make all the features in either Backstitch or Straight Stitch using only 1 strand of floss.

- For the head, nose, neck, arms, legs, and feet, I use a pale, beige-colored floss (such as Anchor shade #378 or DMC shade #841), which is suitable for depicting pale to medium-color skins. For a darker skin color, I recommend Anchor #936 or DMC #632. Getting the color right is crucially important, as it must resemble skin.

- For each eye, make a Straight Stitch about 1⁄16″ long.

- For the nose, make either 1 small Straight Stitch or 2 Straight Stitches perpendicular to each other.

- For the mouth, make 1 small Straight Stitch, about double in size to the length of each eye. To stitch a smiling mouth, make 2 Backstitches.

Embroidery Care

I would advise you to please, please take a little time to stitch up a very quick embroidery sample that you can test wash, dry, and iron. Home appliances can produce extremely varied end results, and what works perfectly for me may well yield completely different results for you.

IRONING

When you iron your finished piece, I recommend avoiding the stitched areas. I find that ironing really flattens the stitches, particularly in heavily filled areas. Try pressing the tip of the iron right up to the stitches, as shown.

If you absolutely must iron over the embroidery, place the piece wrong side up on top of a folded towel and press. Go gently; do not press too hard or for too long, and do not use the steam setting.

WASHING AND DRYING

I find that, in general, all embroideries made with color-fast cotton floss and stitched on cotton fabrics with cotton thread can be washed with care. Wash on a gentle cycle and avoid tumble drying if possible. Line drying is much nicer and will not crease and crinkle the stitched areas as much. Please note it is in the very nature of embroidery that once it is out of the hoop and washed, the stitched areas will crinkle, at least a little.

Embroidering the Projects

This book contains twelve embroidered sewing projects, each with a choice of three alternative embroidery patterns. Before undertaking any of the projects, please take a little time to thoroughly read all the instructions first.

For each project, complete instructions are given for floss colors, numbers of strands to use, and which stitches to use. The purpose of these precise instructions is not to suggest that this is the only way the embroidery can be made, but rather to prescribe one way in which it could be stitched.

In trying out the different projects, I hope you will be able to find your own embroidery "voice" and approach the patterns in your own way. As a beginner, you may choose to follow instructions to the letter. If you're a more experienced stitcher, you may prefer to take the elements you like and change others to suit your own tastes. Embroidery is a very personal journey, and for me, its principal purpose is one of enjoyment. You can choose to keep it simple and complete a pattern in just one kind of embroidery stitch. Or, if you feel in a playful mood, you can introduce some new stitches that you want to try out. Go with your instincts, and you will produce something uniquely "you."

ADDITIONAL PATTERNS

In this book, I wanted to offer as many embroidery design options as possible, so I created many patterns in addition to those for the projects. You'll find them at the back of this book, along with the project embroidery patterns. There's plenty of variety to keep you stitching for a long while yet! These extra patterns do not include stitching instructions, but once you discover the stitches and techniques that you enjoy best, the patterns are there for you to play around with to your heart's content.

Substituting Embroidery Patterns

In any given project, if you want to use an embroidery pattern other than those specified for that project, first measure the height and width of the four suggested embroidery patterns. Make sure that the pattern you wish to substitute is no bigger (and not much smaller) in size than the original.

FLOSS COLORS

The floss colors used in each project pattern are listed under the materials needed for that section. These are simply a list of the colors needed and are not specific shades of any particular brand.

SEWING TOOL KIT

Here are the supplies you'll need to stitch up the projects in this book once you've embroidered them. You need only a few basic sewing tools and supplies, many of which you may already have. All can easily be found in your local quilt shop or fabric store.

Sewing machine   A basic domestic machine that is in good working order and has a zigzag stitch will help you complete the projects quickly and easily.

Sewing thread   I use white, 100% cotton sewing thread for all the projects in this book.

Seam guide tool   If one of these handy little tools didn't come with your machine, you can buy it separately. When fixed to the presser foot, it allows you to quilt straight, even lines, as described in Quilting (page 132).

Sewing pins   Use these pins before basting or tacking to keep fabrics in position as you stitch. I like the long ones with the flat flower heads.

Wide masking tape   Use this to tape down the edges of quilt backing fabric when sandwiching quilted items. Any width 1″–2″ will do the job.

Presser feet   Depending on the make and model of your machine, it probably came with a few different feet specially designed for different sewing tasks. The *regular sewing foot* will allow you to sew straight seams for general sewing and zigzag seams for finishing off raw edges. If your machine has an overcast stitch, you may also have an *overcast foot* to use for finishing off raw edges. The *zipper foot* is designed to allow you to stitch as close as possible to the teeth of a zipper. The *walking or even-feed foot* will come in handy for this book. This foot has an extra set of feed dogs that help your machine evenly feed all the layers of a quilt as you stitch, avoiding puckers and stretching. If you don't have a walking foot, check with your sewing retailer for availability.

Batting   I use cotton batting in all my quilted projects. I use low-loft batting, which has a thickness similar to felt. I would not recommend a higher-loft batting for the projects in this book.

Quilting safety pins For quilting, these are essential for keeping the layers smooth and in place as you stitch. Buy the bent-arm pins rather than the straight ones, as they make it easier to pin through layers.

Rotary cutter; cutting mat; and long, clear plastic ruler These will allow you to cut straight lines with precise measurements. The long ruler is very useful for making long, straight cuts (as when making quilt binding), as well as for marking straight edges.

Creasing tool This is a very handy tool for marking fabric. Instead of leaving an ink mark, it creases the fabric. I mostly use it for marking lines before quilting. I use the Clover Hera Marker. Otherwise, use light pencil marks or a washable or fadeaway fabric marker (always test wash markers before using them).

Fusible interfacing This fabric interfacing has a fusible adhesive on one side. When ironed onto the back of any fabric, it adds a little body. Interfacing can be woven, nonwoven, or knit and is available in different weights. Medium-weight fusible interfacing is used in *A Washing Day Zip Pouch* (page 54). Be sure to read the manufacturer's instructions before applying any interfacing.

Seam ripper Stitching mistakes are bound to happen, so having one of these for quickly pulling out stitches is a big help. I like the ones with the larger handles, simply because it makes them easier to find in a hurry.

Tapestry needle This needle is much thicker than an ordinary sewing needle and has a much bigger eye. It's handy for threading elastic in a project like the *Lost in Stitch Tissue Box Cover* (page 110).

Every stitcher needs a few little pretties on hand for housing those pins, needles, and flosses—all of which need cute "homes" to live in.

LOVELY LITTLE KEEPSAKES

New York Taxi Pincushion • Empire State Building Needle Case
Knit One, Purl One Jar Cozy • A Washing Day Zip Pouch

Finished size: 4½″ × 3½″ (11.4cm × 8.9cm) • *Designed and made by Aneela Hoey*

New York Taxi Pincushion

This project makes a fun homemade souvenir of a bygone visit to the Big Apple.
It's also a great introductory embroidery project.

MATERIALS

• 8″ × 8″ (21cm × 21cm) piece of white cotton fabric • 4″ × 5″ (10cm × 13cm) piece of print fabric
• 4″ × 5″ (10cm × 13cm) piece of batting • Large handful of stuffing • 5″ (13cm) embroidery hoop

EMBROIDERY FLOSS: yellow, gray, dark brown, red, orange

Embroidery

Embroidery pattern is on page 136.

Transfer the pattern onto the center of the 8″ × 8″ white fabric and fix it in the hoop, as described in Embroidery Basics (page 8). Refer to the embroidery guide to embroider the design.

New York Taxi Embroidery Guide

	Element	Color	# of strands	Stitch
Outline	Car	Yellow	6	Backstitch
	Front / Back windows	Gray	2	Backstitch
	Tires	Dark brown	6	Backstitch
	Inner tires	Dark brown	1	Backstitch
Outline and fill	Taillight	Red	6	Backstitch
Embroider	Road / Door edge / Taxi sign	Dark brown	1	Backstitch
	Headlight	Orange	6	Straight Stitch
	Speed marks / Door handles	Dark brown	1	Straight Stitch

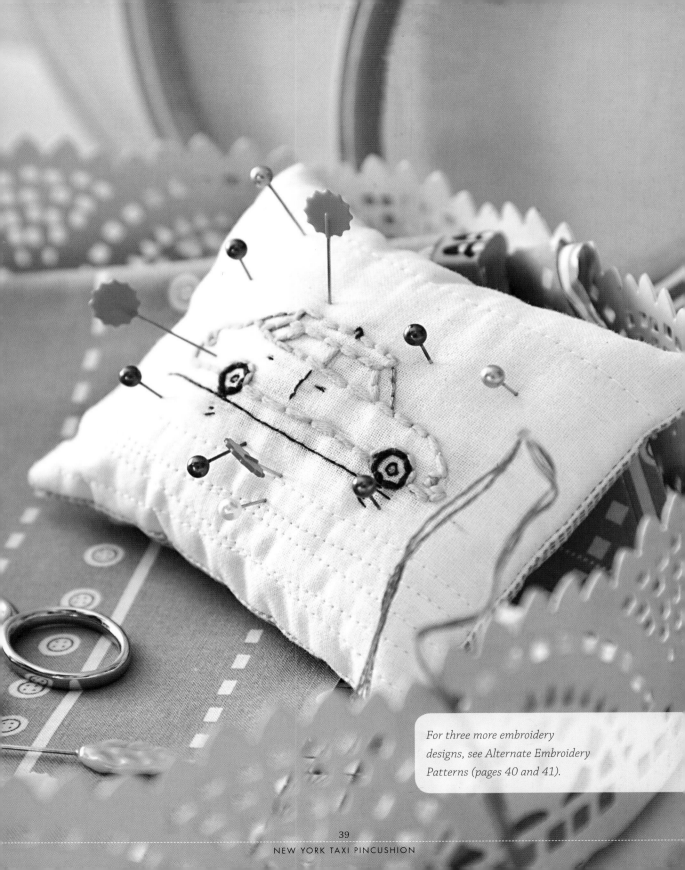

For three more embroidery designs, see Alternate Embroidery Patterns (pages 40 and 41).

Pincushion

1. Remove the embroidery from the hoop and press with an iron, as described in Ironing (page 32), taking care not to iron the embroidered parts.

2. Cut the embroidered fabric down to 5″ wide × 4″ high, keeping the embroidery centered.

3. Place the embroidered fabric right side up on top of the batting and hand baste with a couple of stitches to keep it in place. Set up your sewing machine with a walking foot for quilting and stitch a few random lines across the width above and below the embroidery. Refer to the project photo (page 39) and Quiltmaking Techniques (page 131).

4. Place the embroidered piece and the print fabric right sides together. Pin and baste the edges. Machine stitch all around the outside edge with a ¼″ seam allowance, leaving a 3″ gap at one end. Trim a little of the excess fabric from the corners to reduce bulk (but not too close to the stitching).

5. Turn right side out and fill the pincushion with the stuffing until plump.

6. Refer to Closing Stitches (at right) to hand sew the opening closed.

Alternate Embroidery Patterns

Transfer your chosen pattern onto the center of the 8″ × 8″ white fabric and fix it in the hoop, as described in Embroidery Basics (page 8). Embroider according to the embroidery guide for each pattern. When the embroidery is finished, follow the instructions for Pincushion (above).

CLOSING STITCHES

Use this closing stitch to hand sew openings in pieces like the pincushion.

1. Fold the raw edges inward, the same width as the seam allowance. Finger-press along the folded edges.

2. At one end of the opening, make several small stitches, one on top of the other, to secure the thread end.

3. To make a stitch, insert the needle through both folded edges, close to the folds, and pull it through. Repeat about ⅟₁₆″ away from the first stitch and continue along the opening. Use small, neat stitches, not too far apart, to create a nicely finished closure.

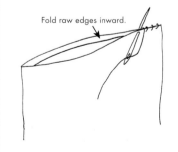

Fold raw edges inward.

Puppy Dog Tails

Embroidery pattern is on page 136.

EMBROIDERY FLOSS: gray, brown, red, dark brown

Puppy Dog Tails Embroidery Guide

	Element	Color	# of strands	Stitch
Outline	Head and body	Gray	2	Running Stitch
Outline and fill	Ear	Brown	6	Backstitch
	Ball	Red	3	Backstitch
Embroider	Nose	Brown	6	French Knot
	Eye	Dark brown	2	French Knot
	Mouth	Brown	2	Straight Stitch

Little Hedgehog

Embroidery pattern is on page 136.

EMBROIDERY FLOSS: beige, brown, medium brown, gray, red, dark brown, white

Little Hedgehog Embroidery Guide

	Element	Color	# of strands	Stitch
Outline	Face/Mouth	Beige	2	Backstitch
	Body	Brown	6	Backstitch
	Feet	Medium brown	2	Backstitch
	Mushroom stem	Gray	1	Backstitch
Outline and fill	Mushroom top	Red	6	Backstitch
Embroider	Eye	Dark brown	1	Backstitch and French Knot
	Nose	Dark brown	3	French Knot
	Spikes	Brown	1	Straight Stitch*
	Large mushroom spots	White	6	French Knot
	Small mushroom spot	White	2	French Knot

* Make 2 straight stitches into an upside down V for each spike.

Sweet Shoes

Embroidery pattern is on page 136.

EMBROIDERY FLOSS: dark brown

Sweet Shoes Embroidery Guide

	Element	Color	# of strands	Stitch
Outline and fill	Shoes	Dark brown	2	Backstitch

Finished size: 3¼ ″ × 4½″ (8.3cm × 11.4cm) • *Designed and made by Aneela Hoey*

Empire State Building Needle Case

Make this on its own or as a coordinating souvenir piece to go with New York Taxi Pincushion *for another bite of the Big Apple. This charming needle case not only looks cute, but it is also useful for keeping your sewing needles separate from your embroidery ones—just pop them onto different pages.*

MATERIALS

- 8″ × 8″ (21cm × 21cm) piece of white cotton fabric • 5″ × 11″ (13cm × 28cm) piece of print fabric
- 4″ × 12″ (10cm × 31cm) piece of orange felt • 5″ × 7″ (13cm × 18cm) piece of batting
- 5″ (13cm) embroidery hoop

EMBROIDERY FLOSS: gray, dark brown, turquoise

Embroidery

Embroidery pattern is on page 137.

Transfer the pattern onto the center of the 8″ × 8″ white fabric and fix it in the hoop, as described in Embroidery Basics (page 8). Refer to the embroidery guide to embroider the design.

Empire State Building Embroidery Guide

	Element	Color	# of strands	Stitch
Outline	Front of building	Gray	2	Backstitch
	Center left edge on front of building	Dark brown	2	Backstitch
	Front windows	Turquoise	1	Straight Stitch
	Top front windows	Gray	1	Straight Stitch
	Spike	Gray	2	Backstitch
Outline and fill	Side of building	Gray	3	Backstitch

For three more embroidery designs, see Alternate Embroidery Patterns (pages 46 and 47).

Needle Case

1. Remove the embroidery from the hoop and press with an iron, as described in Ironing (page 32), taking care not to iron the embroidered parts.

2. Cut the embroidered fabric down to 3¾″ wide × 5″ high, keeping the embroidery centered.

3. For the cover, place the smaller piece of print fabric and the embroidered fabric right sides together, with the wrong side of the embroidered piece uppermost. Make sure that the embroidery is not placed upside down.

4. From the embroidered side, stitch together with a ¼″ seam allowance down the right-hand side. Open out and press the seam open.

5. Place the embroidered fabric / back cover piece right side up on top of the batting and hand baste with a couple stitches to keep it in place. Set up your sewing machine with a walking foot for quilting and stitch a few vertical lines spaced about 1″ apart, avoiding the embroidery. Refer to the project photo (page 43) and Quiltmaking Techniques (page 131).

6. Place the cover and lining right sides together. Pin and baste the edges. Machine stitch all around the outside edge with a ¼″ seam allowance, leaving a 3″ gap along one of the long sides. Trim a little of the excess fabric from the corners to reduce bulk (but not too close to the stitching).

7. Turn the piece right side out and refer to Closing Stitches (page 40) to hand sew the opening closed.

8. Open out the needle case with the lining side uppermost. Place the larger felt rectangle in the middle and the smaller felt rectangle centered on top of that. Machine stitch down the center to attach the pages.

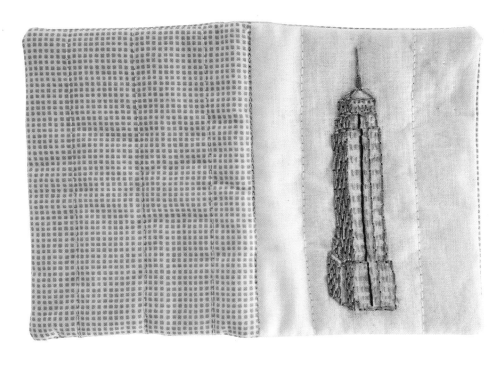

EMPIRE STATE BUILDING NEEDLE CASE

Alternate Embroidery Patterns

Transfer your chosen pattern onto the center of the 8″ × 8″ white fabric and fix it in the hoop, as described in Embroidery Basics (page 8). Embroider according to the embroidery guide for each pattern. When the embroidery is finished, follow the instructions for Needle Case (page 44).

Sleepy Kitty

Embroidery pattern is on page 137.

EMBROIDERY FLOSS: orange, aqua, gray, dark brown

Sleepy Kitty Embroidery Guide

	Element	Color	# of strands	Stitch
Outline	Head and body	Orange	6	Backstitch
	Forehead	Orange	2	Running Stitch
Fill	Inner ears	Aqua	2	Backstitch
Embroider	Whiskers	Gray	1	Backstitch
	Eyes and mouth	Dark brown	1	Backstitch
	Nose	Aqua	6	French Knot
	Toes	Orange	1	Straight Stitch

A Slow Snail

Embroidery pattern is on page 136.

EMBROIDERY FLOSS: red, pink, coral, burgundy, beige

A Slow Snail Embroidery Guide

	Element	Color	# of strands	Stitch
Outline	Head and body	Red	2	Running Stitch
	Shell spiral	Pink	3	Backstitch
Double Outline	Shell	Coral	6	Backstitch
Embroider	Eyes	Burgundy	1	Backstitch
	Nose	Beige	1	Backstitch
	Mouth	Red	1	Backstitch
	Antennae	Burgundy	1	Backstitch
	Antennae tips	Burgundy	3	French Knot

Retro Sunglasses

Embroidery pattern is on page 138.

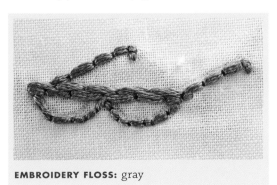

EMBROIDERY FLOSS: gray

Retro Sunglasses Embroidery Guide

	Element	Color	# of strands	Stitch
Outline and fill	Sunglasses	Gray	6	Backstitch

Finished size: 11″ × 4″ (28cm × 10cm) (Fits a jar with a 3½″ / 9cm diameter.)

Designed and made by Aneela Hoey

Knit One, Purl One Jar Cozy

This jar cozy is a fun way to dress up an empty jar and transform it into something pretty to house knitting needles, pens, notions, flowers, or even jam.

MATERIALS

- 7″ × 14″ (18cm × 36cm) piece of white cotton fabric • 5″ × 12″ (13cm × 30.5cm) piece of lining fabric
- 5″ × 12″ (13cm × 30.5cm) piece of batting • 2″ × 3″ (5cm × 8cm) piece of fabric for the fastening loops
- 2 buttons (½″ / 13mm / 20L) • 5″ (13cm) embroidery hoop

EMBROIDERY FLOSS: gray, deep pink, golden yellow, burgundy, orange, brown, aqua

Embroidery

Embroidery pattern is on page 136.

Transfer the pattern onto the center of the 14″ wide × 7″ high white fabric and fix it in the hoop, as described in Embroidery Basics (page 8). Refer to the embroidery guide to embroider the design.

Knit One, Purl One Embroidery Guide

	Element	Color	# of strands	Stitch
Outline	Knitting needles	Gray	2	Backstitch
	Diamond pattern	Deep pink / Golden yellow	6/6	Backstitch
	Dashed lines	Burgundy	2	Running Stitch
Double outline	Knitting	Orange	3	Backstitch
Embroider	Stitches on needles	Orange	3	Backstitch
	Crosses	Brown/Aqua	3/3	Cross-Stitch

For three more embroidery designs, see Alternate Embroidery Patterns (pages 52 and 53).

Jar Cozy

1. Remove the embroidery from the hoop and press with an iron, as described in Ironing (page 32), taking care not to iron the embroidered parts.

2. Cut the embroidered fabric down to 12″ wide × 5″ high, keeping the embroidery centered.

3. Place the embroidered fabric right side up on top of the batting and hand baste with a couple stitches to keep it in place.

4. Cut the fastening loop fabric into 2 strips 1″ × 3″. Refer to Fabric Loops (page 51) to make 2 loops.

5. Position the 2 fabric loops on the left edge of the embroidered fabric as shown, making sure the raw ends of the loops are pointing outward. Hand baste the loops in place.

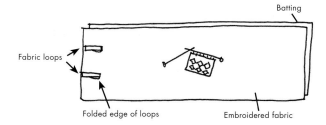

Batting

Fabric loops

Folded edge of loops

Embroidered fabric

6. Place the lining fabric on top, wrong side up. Pin and hand baste in place.

7. Machine stitch with a ½″ seam allowance all around the outside edge, leaving a 5″ gap on one long side.

8. Trim a little of the excess fabric from the corners (not too close to the stitching). Turn the piece right side out. Refer to Closing Stitches (page 40) to hand sew the opening closed.

9. Set up your sewing machine with a walking foot for quilting and stitch a few vertical lines spaced about 1″ apart. Refer to the project

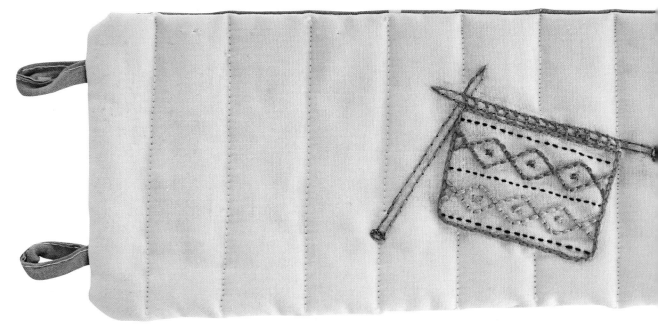

photo (page 50 and below) and Quiltmaking Techniques (page 131).

10. Wrap the cozy around the jar and mark the positions for the buttons with a pencil. Stitch the buttons in place.

TIP

You may wish to avoid machine stitching over embroidered areas. Consider stopping the stitching as you reach the embroidered areas and then continuing just beyond them. Backstitch at the beginning and the end of each line to secure.

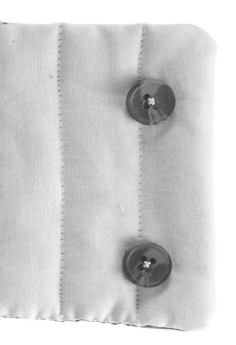

FABRIC LOOPS

Use this method to make the fastening loops for *Knit One, Purl One Jar Cozy* (page 48) and the hanging loop for *Christmas Wrapping Stocking* (page 88). See the individual projects for the cutting dimensions of the fabric strip.

1. Fold the cut fabric strip in half along its length; press. Open it out flat; then fold each long edge toward the central crease and press (Figure A).

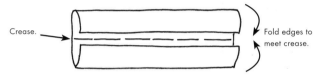

Crease. →   ← Fold edges to meet crease.

Figure A

2. Fold the fabric strip in half again, aligning the 2 long folded edges; press. Topstitch the folded edges together down the length of the strip, a scant $\frac{1}{16}''$ from the folds, backstitching at the beginning and end (Figure B).

Fold in half.

Figure B

3. Fold the strip in half, matching the short ends; press. Hand baste the short ends together with a couple quick stitches (Figure C). The loop is now ready to use in the project.

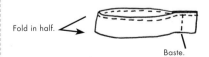

Fold in half. ←

Baste.

Figure C

Alternate Embroidery Patterns

Transfer your chosen pattern onto the center of the 14˝ wide × 7˝ high white fabric and fix it in the hoop, as described in Embroidery Basics (page 8). Embroider according to the embroidery guide for each pattern. When the embroidery is finished, follow the instructions for Jar Cozy (page 50).

Goldfish

Embroidery pattern is on page 139.

EMBROIDERY FLOSS: gray-blue, light aqua, orange, aqua, dark brown

Goldfish Embroidery Guide

	Element	Color	# of strands	Stitch
Outline	Bottom of fishbowl	Gray-blue	4	Running Stitch
	Water line	Light aqua	3	Running Stitch
	Fish	Orange	2	Backstitch
Double outline	Fishbowl	Aqua	6	Backstitch
Embroider	Fish scales	Orange	1	Backstitch
	Tail fin	Orange	1	Straight Stitch
	Bubbles	Light aqua	6	French Knot
	Eye	Dark brown	1	French Knot
	Screw top lines on neck of bowl	Gray-blue	4	Backstitch

A Sailing We Will Go

Embroidery pattern is on page 137.

EMBROIDERY FLOSS: aqua, gray, dark brown, orange, light aqua

A Sailing We Will Go Embroidery Guide

	Element	Color	# of strands	Stitch
Outline	Big sail	Aqua	6	Running Stitch*
	Little sail	Gray	3	Backstitch
	Pole	Gray	6	Backstitch
	Boat	Dark brown	4	Backstitch
Fill	Boat	Dark brown	2	Running Stitch
Outline and fill	Flag	Orange	4	Split Stitch
Embroider	Tip of pole	Gray	6	French Knot
	Lines on big sail	Aqua	1	Backstitch
	Lines on little sail	Light aqua / Orange	6/6	Backstitch
	Sail ropes	Dark brown	1	Backstitch

* Make with alternating long and short stitches.

London Bus

Embroidery pattern is on page 136.

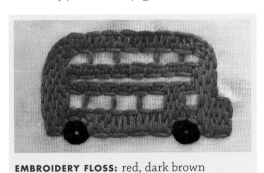

EMBROIDERY FLOSS: red, dark brown

London Bus Embroidery Guide

	Element	Color	# of strands	Stitch
Outline and fill	Bus	Red	6	Backstitch
	Wheels	Dark brown	3	Backstitch

Finished size: 7½″ × 5¼″ (19cm × 13.3cm) • *Designed and made by Aneela Hoey*

A Washing Day Zip Pouch

Use this sturdy little zip pouch yourself to house flosses and scissors while stitching on the go, or make it as a gift for someone else to use—the decision is yours.

MATERIALS

- 11″ × 19″ (28cm × 49cm) piece of white cotton fabric
- 8″ × 12″ (21cm × 31cm) piece of print fabric for lining
- 8″ × 12″ (21cm × 31cm) piece of medium-weight fusible interfacing
- 7″ (18cm) zipper • 8″ (20cm) embroidery hoop

EMBROIDERY FLOSS: beige, dark brown, gray, light aqua, light pink, golden yellow, aqua, red, medium pink

CUTTING

White fabric:

Cut 1 piece 11″ × 11″ for the front.

Cut 1 piece 6″ × 8″ for the back.

Print fabric:

Cut 2 pieces 6″ × 8″.

Interfacing:

Cut 2 pieces 6″ × 8″.

Embroidery

Embroidery pattern is on page 138.

Transfer the pattern onto the center of the 11″ × 11″ white fabric square and fix it in the hoop, as described in Embroidery Basics (page 8).

Note: The sweater and clothespin bag are embroidered, and then decorative stitching is done on top of the embroidery.

For three more embroidery designs, see Alternate Embroidery Patterns (pages 59–61).

A Washing Day Embroidery Guide

	Element	Color	# of strands	Stitch
Outline	Poles	Beige	2	Backstitch
	Washing line	Dark brown	1	Backstitch
	Clothespin bag opening	Gray	6	Backstitch
Outline and fill	Sweater	Light aqua	6	Backstitch
	Socks	Light pink	6	Split Stitch
	Sock heels	Golden yellow	6	Split Stitch
	Clothespin bag	Golden yellow	6	Backstitch
Fill	Scarf stripes	Aqua/Red	6/6	Split Stitch*
	Inside of sweater (seen through neckline)	Light aqua	3	Backstitch
	Sweater neck-line / Cuffs / Hem	Light aqua / Dark brown	3/1	Straight Stitch**
	Inside of clothespin bag	Golden yellow	6	Straight Stitch
Embroider	Scarf tassels	Red	6	French Knot and Straight Stitch
	Clothespin bag hanger	Gray	2	Backstitch
	Clothespins	Red / Golden yellow / Medium pink	6/6/6	Straight Stitch

* Use the special Split Stitch as described in Special Techniques (page 29).
** Work alternate vertical stitches in 3 strands of light aqua and 1 strand of dark brown.

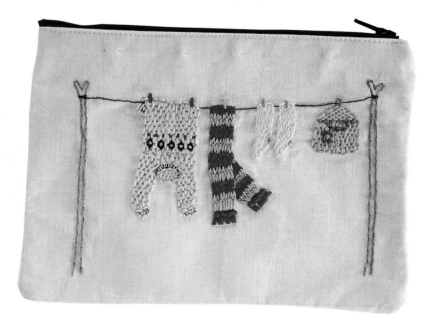

DECORATIVE STITCHES

Follow the guidelines in Special Techniques (page 29) to stitch the decorative patterns on the sweater and the clothespin bag. Use the patterns (below) and the photographs of the finished embroidery, along with the embroidery guides, as references for placement.

SWEATER

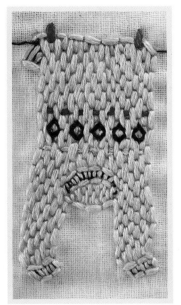

Sweater Decorative Embroidery Guide

	Element	Color	# of strands	Stitch
Embroider	Top row	Red	6	Running Stitch
	Middle row (diamonds)	Dark brown	3	Backstitch
	Bottom row	Golden yellow	6	Running Stitch

CLOTHESPIN BAG

Clothespin Bag Decorative Embroidery Guide

	Element	Color	# of strands	Stitch
Embroider	Flower center	Medium pink	3	French Knot
	Petals	Red	3	French Knot
	Stem and leaves	Light aqua	2	Backstitch

Zip Pouch

1. Remove the embroidery from the hoop and press with an iron, as described in Ironing (page 32), taking care not to iron the embroidered parts.

2. Cut the embroidered fabric down to 8″ wide × 6″ high, keeping the embroidery centered.

3. Follow the manufacturer's instructions to apply one of the fusible interfacing pieces to the back of the embroidery and the other piece to the back of the plain white back.

4. Place the embroidered fabric and one of the lining pieces wrong sides together. Sew together along the top edge, stitching ⅜″ from the edge. Refer to Seam Finishes (page 59) to zigzag or overlock the raw edges to finish them.

5. Repeat Step 4 with the back and the second lining piece.

6. Fold over the top edge ½″ to the lining side on both pieces; press.

7. Attach a zipper foot to your sewing machine. Pin the top folded edge of the embroidered front piece to the left side of the zipper, next to the zipper teeth. Topstitch in place close to the fold. Repeat this step, stitching the back piece to the right side of the zipper.

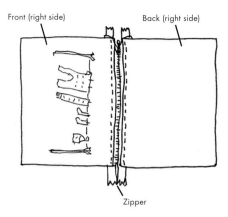

Front (right side) Back (right side)

Zipper

TIP

After stitching the zipper to the pouch front and back, open the zipper halfway. This is very important—otherwise you won't be able to open the pouch after you sew the front and back together.

8. Place the pouch front and back right sides together, with one of the lining sides facing up. With a rotary cutter and ruler, trim the side and bottom edges of all layers a little to even them up before stitching them together.

9. Pin and hand baste the side and bottom edges. Machine stitch them together with a ¼″ seam allowance.

10. Refer to Seam Finishes (page 59) to zigzag or overlock the raw edges of the seams together to finish them; then turn the pouch right sides out.

Use these seam finishes to finish raw edges where indicated for *A Washing Day Zip Pouch* (page 54) and *Christmas Wrapping Stocking* (page 88). See the individual projects for seam finishing instructions.

Most domestic sewing machines come with a zigzag stitch as a standard feature. You may need to change the presser foot on your machine, so check your machine's manual.

Set the zigzag to a stitch width of about ¼″ (5mm) and the stitch length (if possible) to about ¼″ (5mm).

If your machine comes with an overlock stitch, use this instead. You may also be able to sew seams and overlock in one step, which is a real time-saver. You may need to attach an overlock foot first, so check your machine's manual.

Alternate Embroidery Patterns

Transfer your chosen pattern onto the center of the 11″ × 11″ white fabric and fix it in the hoop, as described in Embroidery Basics (page 8). Embroider according to the embroidery guide for each pattern. When the embroidery is finished, follow the instructions for Zip Pouch (page 58).

Hoot the Owl

Embroidery pattern is on page 137.

EMBROIDERY FLOSS: deep pink, burgundy, light pink, medium pink, red

Hoot the Owl Embroidery Guide

	Element	Color	# of strands	Stitch
Outline	Body	Deep pink / Burgundy	6/1	Couching Stitch
	Wings	Light pink	6	Backstitch
	Eyes	Burgundy	2	Backstitch
Outline and fill	Pupils	Medium pink	4	Backstitch
	Nose	Red	6	Backstitch
	Inner ears	Light pink	3	Backstitch
Fill	Wings	Light pink	6	French Knot
Embroider	Tummy feathers	Deep pink	3	Backstitch
	Legs and feet	Burgundy	1	Backstitch

Bicycle Girl

Embroidery pattern is on page 139.

EMBROIDERY FLOSS: beige, aqua, gray, dark brown, pale yellow, orange, light pink, light aqua, red

Bicycle Girl Embroidery Guide

	Element	Color	# of strands	Stitch
Outline	Face / Neck / Hands / Legs / Nose	Beige	1	Backstitch
	Wheels	Aqua/Gray	6/1	Couching Stitch
	Collar/Pocket	Dark brown	2	Backstitch
	Wheel spokes	Gray	1	Backstitch
	Pedal wheel	Gray	2	Backstitch
	Pedal arm	Aqua	2	Backstitch
	Pedal	Gray	3	Backstitch
Outline and fill	Hair	Pale yellow	3	Backstitch
	Dress	Orange	6	Backstitch
	Bicycle frame	Light pink	6	Backstitch
	Seat	Light aqua	3	Backstitch
	Shoes	Dark brown	2	Backstitch
Fill	Pocket/Collar	Orange	6	Straight Stitch
Embroider	Eyes	Dark brown	2	French Knot
	Mouth	Red	1	Backstitch

Big Chick, Little Chicks

Embroidery pattern is on page 137.

EMBROIDERY FLOSS: light pink, red, burgundy, orange, medium pink, coral, pale yellow

Big Chick, Little Chicks Embroidery Guide

Embroider	Element	Color	# of strands	Stitch
Big chick				
	Body	Light pink/Red	6/1	Couching Stitch
	Wing	Red	2	Running Stitch
	Eye	Burgundy	2	French Knot
	Beak	Orange	6	Backstitch
	Legs and feet	Burgundy	1	Backstitch
Little chick (middle)				
	Body	Medium pink	4	Backstitch
	Wing	Coral	2	Running Stitch
	Eye	Burgundy	1	French Knot
	Beak	Orange	2	Backstitch
	Legs and feet	Burgundy	1	Backstitch
Little chick (right)				
	Body	Orange	4	Split Stitch
	Wing	Coral	2	Running Stitch
	Eye	Burgundy	1	French Knot
	Beak	Pale yellow	2	Backstitch
	Legs and feet	Burgundy	1	Backstitch

STITCHED WITH LOVE
TO GIVE

My Favorite Hobby Horse Cushion Cover • Row, Row Your Boat Patchwork Cushion Cover
Let's Go Fly a Kite Baby Quilt • Christmas Wrapping Stocking

If there is any feeling better than stitching up
something pretty to use for yourself, it has to
be the feeling you get when you stitch up a little
something lovely for someone else (with a little
love in every stitch you take).

Finished size: 14″ × 14″ (36cm × 36cm) • *Designed and made by Aneela Hoey*

My Favorite Hobby Horse Cushion Cover

Here's a perfectly pretty cover to dress up a cushion for a little girl you might know. The inspiration for this piece was a second-hand hobbyhorse my daughter purchased for about 75 cents at a tag sale a few years ago.

MATERIALS

- 1 yard (0.9m) of white cotton fabric • 14″ × 14″ (36cm × 36cm) cushion form
- 7″ (18cm) embroidery hoop

EMBROIDERY FLOSS: beige, light aqua, red, dark brown, light brown, medium brown, golden yellow, aqua

CUTTING

White fabric:

Cut 1 piece 17″ × 17″ for the cushion front.

Cut 2 pieces 12″ × 15½″ for the cushion back.

Embroidery

Embroidery pattern is on page 139.

Transfer the pattern onto the center of the 17″ × 17″ white fabric and fix it in the hoop, as described in Embroidery Basics (page 8). Refer to the embroidery guide (page 67) to embroider the design.

Note: The girl's dress is embroidered, and then decorative stitching is done on top of the embroidery.

For three more embroidery designs, see Alternate Embroidery Patterns (pages 69–71).

DECORATIVE STITCHES

Follow the guidelines in Special Techniques (page 29) to stitch the decorative trim on the dress. Use the pattern (below) and the photographs of the finished embroidery as references for placement.

My Favorite Hobby Horse Embroidery Guide

	Element	Color	# of strands	Stitch
Outline	Girl's face / Nose / Arms / Legs / Hand	Beige	1	Backstitch
Outline and fill	Dress	Light aqua	6	Backstitch
	Jacket	Red	4	Split stitch
	Hair band	Red	6	Backstitch
	Hair	Dark brown	3	Backstitch
	Shoes	Light aqua	2	Backstitch
	Horse's head	Light brown	6	Scatter Stitch
	Horse's mane	Medium brown	6	Scatter Stitch
	Horse body (stick)	Golden yellow	6	Backstitch
	Bridle	Aqua	4	Backstitch
Embroider	Girl's eyes	Dark brown	1	Straight Stitch
	Girl's mouth	Red	1	Straight Stitch
	Horse's eye	Dark brown	6	French Knot
	Dress trim	Red	2	Backstitch*

* Use stitching pattern (at left) and follow the instructions in Special Techniques (page 29).

CUSHION COVER

1. Remove the embroidery from the hoop and press with an iron, as described in Ironing (page 32), taking care not to iron the embroidered parts.

2. Cut the embroidered fabric down to 15½″ × 15½″, keeping the embroidery centered.

3. On one of the cushion back pieces, fold over a long edge ¼″ to the wrong side; press. Fold it over another ½″; press. Repeat this step with the second back piece.

4. Topstitch the folded edges on both pieces ⅜″ from the outer edge.

5. Place the embroidered cushion front wrong side up on a flat surface. Place one of the back pieces on top, right side up, aligning it with the top, bottom, and right edges of the cushion front. The folded edge should cover the center of the cushion front.

6. Place the second back piece on top, right side up, aligning it with the top, bottom, and left edges of the cushion front. The folded edge should overlap the first back piece.

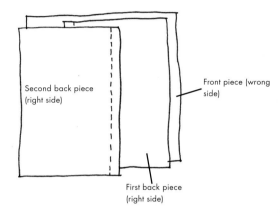

Second back piece (right side)

Front piece (wrong side)

First back piece (right side)

7. Pin and hand baste the edges together. Machine stitch all around the outside edge with a ¼˝ seam allowance. Trim a little of the excess fabric from the corners to reduce bulk (but not too close to the stitching).

8. Turn the cover inside out, making sure to turn out and press the sides and corners well.

9. Stitch all around the outside edge with a ½˝ seam allowance.

10. Turn right side out and press, taking care not to iron the embroidered parts. Insert the cushion form.

Alternate Embroidery Patterns

Transfer your chosen pattern onto the center of the 17″ × 17″ white fabric and fix it in the hoop, as described in Embroidery Basics (page 8). Embroider according to the embroidery guide for each pattern. When the embroidery is finished, follow the instructions for Cushion Cover (page 67).

Nutty the Squirrel

Embroidery pattern is on page 136.

EMBROIDERY FLOSS: red, coral, medium pink, burgundy, light pink, brown

Nutty the Squirrel Embroidery Guide

	Element	Color	# of strands	Stitch
	Tail	Red	1	Running Stitch
Outline	Left ear	Coral	2	Backstitch
	Nut	Medium pink	3	Backstitch
Double outline	Head and body	Coral	6	Backstitch
	Nose	Medium pink	3	French Knot
Embroider	Whiskers	Burgundy	1	Backstitch
	Inner ear	Light pink	6	Backstitch
	Eye	Brown	2	French Knot

Bird on a Mushroom

Embroidery pattern is on page 139.

EMBROIDERY FLOSS: light aqua, gray, golden yellow, red, light pink, dark brown, brown, aqua

Bird on a Mushroom Embroidery Guide

	Element	Color	# of strands	Stitch
	Bird	Light aqua	6	Split Stitch
Outline	Mushroom stem	Gray	1	Running Stitch
	Beak	Golden yellow	6	Backstitch
Double outline	Mushroom top	Red	6	Backstitch
Fill	Bird	Light aqua	3	Running Stitch
Embroider	Mushroom spots	Light pink	6	French Knot
	Center line on beak	Dark brown	1	Straight Stitch
	Eye	Brown	3	French Knot
	Grass	Aqua	6	Straight Stitch

A Bunch of Balloons

Embroidery pattern is on page 140.

EMBROIDERY FLOSS: red, aqua, gray, light aqua, light green, dark brown

A Bunch of Balloons Embroidery Guide

	Element	Color	# of strands	Stitch
Outline	Balloons	Red / Aqua / Gray / Light aqua / Light green	6 of each	Backstitch
	Strings	Dark brown	1	Backstitch

Finished size: 14″ × 14″ (36cm × 36cm) • *Designed and made by Aneela Hoey*

Row, Row Your Boat Patchwork Cushion Cover

This project features embroidery stitched on a pale, solid-colored fabric. For best results on the patchwork, choose prints that blend well with the solid fabric and the floss colors used.

MATERIALS

- 12″ × 12″ (30cm × 30cm) piece of solid-colored cotton fabric • 12 squares 4¼″ × 4¼″ (10.8cm × 10.8cm) of assorted print fabrics • 16″ × 24″ (41cm × 61cm) piece of cotton fabric for cushion back • 14″ × 14″ (36cm × 36cm) cushion form • 8″ (20cm) embroidery hoop

EMBROIDERY FLOSS: orange, pale yellow, gray, turquoise, beige, golden yellow, teal blue, dark brown, red, sea green

CUTTING

Cushion back fabric:

Cut 2 pieces 12″ × 15½″.

Embroidery

Embroidery pattern is on page 140.

Transfer the pattern onto the center of the 12″ × 12″ solid-colored cotton fabric and fix it in the hoop, as described in Embroidery Basics (page 8). Refer to the embroidery guide (page 74) to embroider the design.

For three more embroidery designs, see Alternate Embroidery Patterns (pages 76 and 77).

Row, Row Your Boat Embroidery Guide

	Element	Color	# of strands	Stitch
Outline	Sweater	Orange	6	Split Stitch
	Collar	Pale yellow	3	Backstitch
	Boat	Gray/Orange	6/1	Couching Stitch
	Seat	Gray	2	Backstitch
	Oars	Turquoise	3	Running Stitch
	Nose/Face/Neck/Hands	Beige	1	Backstitch
Outline and fill	Hair	Golden yellow	3	Split Stitch
	Trousers	Teal blue	6	Backstitch
Embroider	Pattern on sweater	Dark brown	2	Backstitch
	Boat panels (outside)	Gray	1	Backstitch
	Boat panels (inside)	Gray	6	Backstitch
	Mooring ring (at front of boat)	Pale yellow	6	Backstitch
	Eyes	Dark brown	1	Straight Stitch
	Mouth	Red	1	Straight Stitch
	Waves	Sea green	2	Backstitch and Running Stitch

Cushion Cover

All seams are ¼″ unless otherwise noted.

CUSHION FRONT

1. Remove the embroidery from the hoop and press with an iron, as described in Ironing (page 32), taking care not to iron the embroidered parts.

2. Cut the embroidered fabric down to 8″ × 8″, keeping the embroidery centered.

3. Select 2 of the print fabric squares; with right sides facing, stitch them together along one edge. Repeat this step with a second pair of squares. Press the seams to one side.

4. Stitch one pair of squares to the top of the embroidered fabric and the other pair to the bottom. Press the seams toward the squares.

5. Stitch the remaining squares into 2 rows of 4 squares each. Press the seams to one side.

6. Stitch the rows to either side of the embroidered/patchwork center. Press the seams toward the squares. Press the cushion front, making sure not to iron the embroidered parts.

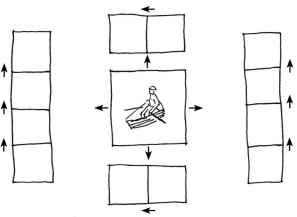

Assembly diagram

ASSEMBLY

1. On one of the cushion back pieces, fold over a long edge ¼˝ to the wrong side; press. Fold it over another ½˝; press. Repeat this step with the second back piece.

2. Topstitch along the folded edges of both pieces ⅜˝ from the outer edge.

3. Place the embroidered cushion front right side up on a flat surface. Place one of the back pieces on top, wrong side up and aligned with the top, bottom, and left edges of the cushion front. The folded edge should cover the center of the cushion front.

4. Place the second back piece on top, wrong side up, aligning it with the top, bottom, and right edges of the cushion front. The folded edge should overlap the first back piece.

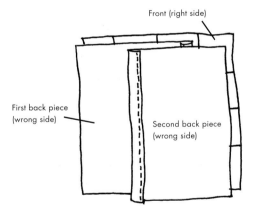

Front (right side)

First back piece
(wrong side)

Second back piece
(wrong side)

5. Pin and hand baste the edges together. Machine stitch all around the outside edge with a ¾˝ seam allowance.

6. Refer to Seam Finishes (page 59) to zigzag or overlock the raw edges to finish the seam.

7. Turn right side out and press, taking care not to iron the embroidered parts. Insert the cushion form.

Alternate Embroidery Patterns

Transfer your chosen pattern onto the center of the 12″ × 12″ solid-colored cotton fabric and fix it in the hoop, as described in Embroidery Basics (page 8). Embroider according to the embroidery guide for each pattern. When the embroidery is finished, follow the instructions for Cushion Cover (page 74).

Nine-Patch Sampler

Embroidery pattern is on page 138.

EMBROIDERY FLOSS: brown, beige, medium brown, golden yellow, dark brown

Nine-Patch Sampler Embroidery Guide

	Element	Color	# of strands	Stitch
Top row: Left to right				
Outline	Square 1	Brown	1	Running Stitch
	Square 2	Beige	6	Backstitch
	Square 3	Medium brown	6	Split Stitch
Middle row: Left to right				
Outline	Square 1	Beige	6	Running Stitch*
	Square 2	Medium brown	6	French Knot
	Square 3	Golden yellow / Dark brown	6/1	Couching Stitch
Bottom row: Left to right				
Double outline	Square 1	Golden yellow	6	Backstitch
	Square 2	Dark brown	1	Running Stitch
Outline	Square 3 (outer line)	Medium brown	4	Backstitch
	Square 3 (inner line)	Medium brown	1	Running Stitch

* Use alternating long and short stitches.

A Holiday Snow Globe

Embroidery pattern is on page 143.

EMBROIDERY FLOSS: aqua, gray, red, dark brown, light green, light pink

A Holiday Snow Globe Embroidery Guide

	Element	Color	# of strands	Stitch
	Globe	Aqua	3	Running Stitch
	Base	Gray	6	Backstitch
	House	Gray	2	Backstitch
	Roof	Red	6	Backstitch
Outline	Roof tiles	Red	1	Backstitch
	Chimney	Red	2	Backstitch
	Smoke	Gray	3	Backstitch
	Windows	Dark brown	1	Backstitch
	Hill	Light green	1	Backstitch
	Path	Gray	1	Running Stitch
Outline and fill	Trees	Light green	6	Scatter Stitch
	Door	Red	6	Backstitch
Embroider	Snow	Light pink	6	French Knot
	Doorknob	Dark brown	1	French Knot

Sweet Little Apple Tree

Embroidery pattern is on page 140.

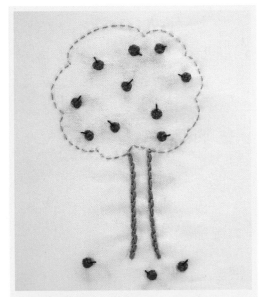

EMBROIDERY FLOSS: coral, medium pink, red, burgundy

Sweet Little Apple Tree Embroidery Guide

	Element	Color	# of strands	Stitch
Outline	Treetop	Coral	2	Running Stitch
Double outline	Tree trunk	Medium pink	6	Backstitch
Outline and fill	Apples	Red	6	Backstitch
Embroider	Apple stems	Burgundy	1	Straight Stitch

Finished size: 35½″ × 39″ (90.2cm × 99.1cm) • *Designed and made by Aneela Hoey*

Let's Go Fly a Kite Baby Quilt

This charming baby quilt combines embroidery with a sweet patchwork border made from half-square triangles. Use printed fabric squares from a precut fabric pack, such as a charm pack, or cut them from scraps or yardage.

MATERIALS

- 1½ yards (1.5m) of white cotton fabric • 22 different prints, each cut 5″ × 5″ (12.7cm × 12.7cm), or a 5″ × 5″ (12.7cm × 12.7cm) precut pack
- 40″ × 44″ (102cm × 112cm) piece of print fabric for backing
- 40″ × 44″ (102cm × 112cm) piece of batting
- ½ yard (0.5m) of fabric for binding • 10″ (25cm) embroidery hoop

EMBROIDERY FLOSS: beige, dark brown, red, aqua, brown, gray, gold, teal, green, light aqua

CUTTING

White fabric:

Cut 2 strips 5½″ × 40″.

Cut 2 strips 5½″ × 26″.

Cut 1 square 22″ × 22″.

Binding fabric:

Cut 5 strips 2½″ × 40″.

Embroidery

Embroidery pattern is on page 141.

Transfer the pattern onto the center of the 22″ × 22″ white fabric and fix it in the hoop, as described in Embroidery Basics (page 8). Refer to the embroidery guide (page 80) to embroider the design.

For three more embroidery designs, see Alternate Embroidery Patterns (pages 84–87).

Let's Go Fly a Kite Embroidery Guide

	Element	Color	# of strands	Stitch
Outline	Face/Neck/Hands	Beige	1	Backstitch
	Eye	Dark brown	1	Backstitch
	Mouth	Red	1	Backstitch
	Kite string	Dark brown	1	Backstitch
	Tail bow string	Aqua	2	Backstitch
Outline and fill	Hair	Brown	3	Backstitch
	Sweater	Red	6	Split Stitch
	Trousers	Gray	6	Backstitch
	Shoes	Dark brown	6	Backstitch
	Kite	Aqua/Gold	6	Backstitch
	Tail bows	Teal/Green/Light aqua	3/3/3	Backstitch

Quilt Top

All seams are ¼″ unless otherwise noted.

1. Remove the embroidery from the hoop and press with an iron, as described in Ironing (page 32), taking care not to iron the embroidered parts.

2. Cut the embroidered piece down to 17″ wide × 21″ high.

3. To make the half-square triangles for the patchwork border, sort the 5″ × 5″ squares into pairs. Take the first pair and place the 2 pieces right sides together. With a pencil, draw a diagonal line from corner to corner on the wrong side of the top square. Machine stitch down each side, ¼″ away from the drawn line. Repeat this step with the remaining pairs of squares.

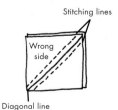

Stitching lines

Wrong side

Diagonal line

4. Cut each square apart along the diagonal line and press the seams to one side.

5. Take 4 of the stitched squares and sew them into a horizontal row, making sure all the triangles face the same direction. Repeat with a second set of 4. Press the seams to one side. Refer to the assembly diagram (below).

6. Referring to the assembly diagram, stitch one row to the top edge of the embroidered fabric and the other to the bottom edge. Press the seams toward the patchwork. Trim the side edges even with the embroidered fabric.

7. Sew the remaining squares into 2 vertical rows of 7 squares each, making sure all of the triangles face in the same direction. Press the seams to one side.

TIP

The first two rows will be placed horizontally on the quilt top, and the third and fourth rows will be placed vertically. If you are using directional prints, you may want to make sure they are all placed facing the right way up before stitching them together.

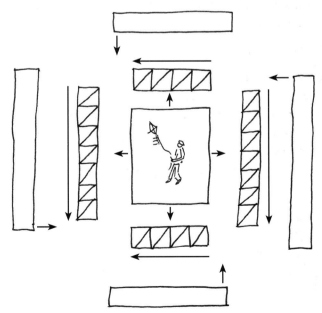

Assembly diagram

8. Stitch a row to each side edge of the quilt top. Press the seams toward the patchwork. Trim the top and bottom edges even with the quilt top.

9. Stitch one 5½″ × 26″ white strip to the top edge of the quilt top and the other to the bottom edge. Press the seams toward the patchwork. Trim the side edges even with the quilt top.

10. Stitch a 5½″ × 40″ white strip to each side of the quilt top. Press the seams toward the patchwork. Trim the top and bottom edges even with the quilt top.

QUILTING AND FINISHING

1. Refer to Quiltmaking Techniques (page 131) to sandwich and baste the quilt top, batting, and backing and to complete the following steps.

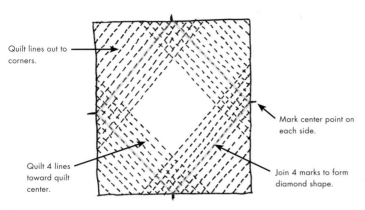

Quilt lines out to corners.

Mark center point on each side.

Quilt 4 lines toward quilt center.

Join 4 marks to form diamond shape.

Quilting diagram

2. Set up your sewing machine with a walking foot for quilting. Using a creasing tool or pencil, lightly mark the center point of each of the quilt's 4 sides. Using the same marker and a ruler, join the 4 marks to make a diamond shape. Quilt along these 4 lines.

3. Attach a seam guide tool to your sewing machine and set it at 1½˝ from the stitching line. From each of the stitched lines, sew 4 parallel lines toward the center of the quilt.

4. Continue to quilt parallel lines out to the corners of the quilt from each of the 4 originally marked lines. Trim the batting and backing even with the quilt top edges.

5. Make and attach double-fold binding to finish the quilt.

Alternate Embroidery Patterns

Transfer your chosen pattern onto the center of the 22″ × 22″ white fabric and fix it in the hoop, as described in Embroidery Basics (page 8). Embroider according to the embroidery guide for each pattern. When the embroidery is finished, follow the instructions for Quilt Top (page 80).

Little Red Riding Hood

Embroidery pattern is on page 141.

EMBROIDERY FLOSS: beige, gray, red, dark brown, white, teal blue

Little Red Riding Hood Embroidery Guide

	Element	Color	# of strands	Stitches
Outline	Nose / Chin / Hands / Legs / Feet	Beige	1 of each	Backstitch
	Dress	Gray	2	Backstitch
	Mushroom stems	Gray	1	Backstitch
Outline and fill	Cape	Red	6	Split Stitch
	Hair	Dark brown	3	Backstitch
	Shoes	Dark brown	2	Backstitch
	Mushroom tops	Red	6	Split Stitch
Embroider	Bow on cape	Red	6	Split Stitch
	Bow knot	Red	6	French Knot
	Mushroom spots	White	2	French Knot
	Eyes	Dark brown	1	Backstitch
	Mouth	Red	1	Backstitch
	Dress hem pattern	Teal blue	3	Backstitch

Cherry on the Tree Swing

Embroidery pattern is on page 142.

Note: This is the embroidery that inspired the *Girl on a Tree Swing* fabric from my Sherbet Pips fabric line for Moda.

EMBROIDERY FLOSS: gray, teal blue, beige, red, dark brown

Cherry on the Tree Swing Embroidery Guide

	Element	Color	# of strands	Stitches
Outline	Tree	Gray	3	Backstitch
	Leaves	Teal blue	3	Backstitch
	Face / Neck / Legs / Hands	Beige	1	Backstitch
	Socks	Gray	1	Backstitch
	Collar and button tab on dress	Red	6	Backstitch
	Swing seat	Gray	6	Backstitch
	Swing ropes	Gray	6	Chain Stitch
Outline and fill	Hair	Dark brown	6	Backstitch
	Dress	Red	6	Backstitch
	Shoes	Dark brown	3	Backstitch
Embroider	Cherries	Red	4	French Knot
	Cherry stems	Dark brown	1	Backstitch
	Front loop of hair bow	Red	6	Backstitch
	Back loop of hair bow	Red	1	Backstitch
	Hair bow knot	Red	4	French Knot
	Dress buttons	Dark brown	2	French Knot
	Eyes	Dark brown	1	Straight Stitch
	Nose	Beige	1	Straight Stitch
	Mouth	Red	1	Straight Stitch
	Top knot of swing ropes	Gray	4	French Knot
	Ferns	Teal blue	2	Backstitch

Scoot

Embroidery pattern is on page 143.

Note: The girl's sweater is embroidered, and then decorative stitching is done on top of the embroidery. This pattern developed from an image in my head of my youngest daughter, Ciara, on her scooter. Scoot was eventually turned into a fabric design for my Sherbet Pips line.

EMBROIDERY FLOSS: beige, dark brown, gray, light aqua, red, aqua, golden yellow, pale biscuit

Scoot Embroidery Guide

	Element	Color	# of strands	Stitch
Outline	Girl's face	Beige	1	Backstitch
	Puppy	Beige	1	Backstitch
	Puppy's ears	Dark brown	1	Backstitch
	Skirt pocket	Gray	1	Backstitch
	Scooter handles and side of base	Gray	6	Backstitch
Outline and fill	Hair	Dark brown	4	Split Stitch
	Sweater	Light aqua	6	Split Stitch
	Scarf stripes	Red/Aqua	6/6	Split Stitch*
	Skirt (not inside pocket)	Golden yellow	6	Backstitch
	Mittens	Red	6	Split Stitch
	Shoes	Dark brown	6	Split Stitch
	Tights	Gray	6	Split Stitch
	Scooter wheels	Dark brown	2	Split Stitch
	Spots on puppy	Dark brown	2	Split Stitch
Fill	Scooter	Pale biscuit	6	Satin Stitch
	Skirt pocket	Golden yellow	6	Backstitch
Embroider	Scarf tassels	Red	6	French Knot and Straight Stitch
	Girl's eye	Dark brown	1	Straight Stitch
	Puppy's eye	Dark brown	1	French Knot
	Puppy's mouth	Dark brown	1	Backstitch
	Puppy's tongue	Red	6	Straight Stitch
	Puppy's nose	Dark brown	3	French Knot
	Scooter shadow	Dark brown	1	Backstitch

* Use the special Split Stitch as described in Special Techniques (page 29).

DECORATIVE STITCHES

Follow the guidelines in Special Techniques (page 29) to stitch the decorative pattern on the sweater. Use the pattern (below) and the photograph of the finished embroidery as references for placement.

SWEATER PATTERN		

Sweater Pattern Embroidery Guide

	Element	Color	# of strands	Stitch
Embroider	Top row	Golden yellow	2	Running Stitch
	Middle row	Dark brown	2	Cross-Stitch
	Bottom row	Red	2	Running Stitch

Finished size: Approximately 11″ × 12½″ (28cm × 32cm) • *Designed and made by Aneela Hoey*

Christmas Wrapping Stocking

*Every Christmas needs a stocking! Hang this sweet number on
Christmas Eve and wait for Santa to notice.*

MATERIALS

• 16″ × 16″ (41cm × 41cm) piece of white cotton fabric • ½ yard (0.5m) of printed fabric
for back and lining • 15″ × 30″ (38.1cm × 76cm) piece of batting • 13″ × 15″ (33cm × 38.1cm) piece of
thin cardboard • 7″ (18cm) embroidery hoop

EMBROIDERY FLOSS: orange, aqua, golden yellow, beige, dark brown, red

CUTTING

Print fabric:

Cut 3 pieces 13″ × 15″ for
the back and lining.

Cut 1 strip 2″ × 9″ for
the hanging loop.

Batting:

Cut 2 pieces 13″ × 15″.

Stocking Pattern

1. Enlarge and copy the Christmas Wrapping Stocking template
pattern (page 93). Cut out the pattern. With a pencil, trace
around the edge onto the thin cardboard to make a stocking
template.

2. Place the top edge of the template less than 1″ from the top
edge of the 16″ × 16″ white fabric, centering it across the width.
Trace the stocking shape with a pencil onto the fabric. Do not
cut the stocking out yet!

For three more embroidery
designs, see Alternate Embroidery
Patterns (pages 94 and 95).

Embroidery

Embroidery pattern is on page 141.

1. Place the embroidery pattern inside the drawn stocking shape toward the bottom right, at least 2˝ from the bottom and right side edges. Refer to the photograph of the finished embroidery for placement.

2. Transfer the pattern to the fabric and fix it in the hoop, as described in Embroidery Basics (page 8). Refer to the embroidery guide to embroider the design.

Christmas Wrapping Embroidery Guide

	Element	Color	# of strands	Stitch
Outline	Coat	Orange	6	Backstitch
	Pockets	Orange	3	Backstitch
	Hat	Aqua	3	Backstitch
	Scarf stripes	Aqua / Golden yellow	6/6	Backstitch
	Face / Hands / Legs / Feet	Beige	1	Backstitch
Outline and fill	Hair	Dark brown	3	Backstitch
	Shoes	Dark brown	2	Backstitch
Fill	Bobble on hat	Golden yellow	2	Straight Stitch
Embroider	Buttons	Dark brown	2	French Knot
	Eyes	Dark brown	1	Straight Stitch
	Nose	Beige	1	Straight Stitch
	Mouth	Red	1	Straight Stitch
	Scarf tassels	Golden yellow	6	Straight Stitch

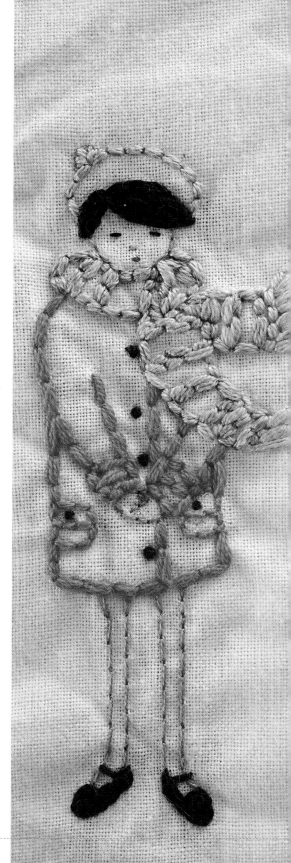

Stocking

All seam allowances are ¼″ unless otherwise noted.

FRONT AND BACK

1. Remove the embroidery from the hoop and press with an iron, as described in Ironing (page 32), taking care not to iron the embroidered parts.

2. Cut the embroidered fabric on the drawn line of the stocking along the top edge only.

3. Trim the remaining sides so that the fabric measures 13″ × 15″; be sure not to cut through the drawn stocking shape.

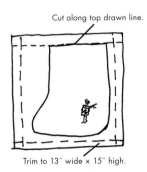

Cut along top drawn line.

Trim to 13″ wide × 15″ high.

4. To make the stocking front, place the embroidered fabric right side up on a flat surface. Place a lining piece on top, wrong side up, and then place a batting piece uppermost. Align the top edges of all 3 layers before proceeding.

5. Pin and machine stitch the layers together across the top edge only, using a ¼″ seam allowance.

6. Flip the batting and lining over the top edge to the back, so that the embroidered fabric is now uppermost. Press the top edge. Pin and baste the 3 layers together and cut around the stocking shape.

7. To make the stocking back, flip the stocking template over and trace it onto the right side of one of the print fabric pieces, lining up the top edge of the template with the top edge of the fabric.

8. Refer to Fabric Loops (page 51) to make a hanging loop from the 2″ × 9″ print fabric strip.

9. Place the hanging loop ¾″ in from the top left corner of the drawn stocking shape, with the folded edge of the loop pointing in at an angle toward the center. Hand baste the loop to secure it.

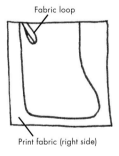

Fabric loop

Print fabric (right side)

10. Top with the remaining lining piece, wrong side up, and the remaining batting piece, placed uppermost. Refer to Steps 5 and 6 to complete the stocking back.

QUILTING AND FINISHING

1. Referring to the quilting diagram as a guide, mark straight lines in a wonky grid pattern on the stocking front using a creasing tool and ruler. Mark the first lines around the embroidery to avoid having to stitch through it. Repeat for the stocking back.

Quilting diagram

TIP

As an alternative to marking or creasing quilting lines, use a strip of masking tape. Stick the strip across the stocking shape and stitch alongside it. Remove and restick the tape for the next line, and continue.

2. Pin to hold the layers together. Set up your sewing machine with a walking foot for quilting and refer to Quiltmaking Techniques (page 131) to quilt the stocking front along the marked lines. Repeat for the stocking back.

ASSEMBLY

1. Place the stocking front and back pieces right sides together. Pin along the side and bottom edges; baste.

2. Machine stitch around the side and bottom edges, using a ½˝ seam allowance and back-stitching at the beginning and the end. Do not stitch across the top edge!

3. Refer to Seam Finishes (page 59) to zigzag or overlock the raw edges to finish them. Clip the curved top of the foot, taking care not to cut too close to the stitching line.

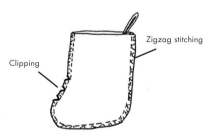

Clipping

Zigzag stitching

4. Turn the stocking right side out and press, taking care not to iron the embroidered parts.

Christmas Wrapping Stocking

Trace template this side up,
onto right side of embroidered fabric.

Flip template over and trace onto
right side of one print fabric piece.

Enlarge 200%.

Alternate Embroidery Patterns

Follow the Stocking Pattern and Embroidery instructions for *Christmas Wrapping Stocking* (page 88) to prepare the template and to position your chosen embroidery pattern. Transfer the pattern and fix it in the hoop, as described in Embroidery Basics (page 8). Embroider according to the embroidery guide for each pattern. When the embroidery is finished, follow the remaining instructions for Stocking (page 91).

Snowy Scene

Embroidery pattern is on page 143.

EMBROIDERY FLOSS: red, dark brown, gray, brown, golden yellow, light aqua, dark green, turquoise, pale pink

Snowy Scene Embroidery Guide

	Element	Color	# of strands	Stitches
Outline	House	Red	3	Running Stitch
	Windows	Dark brown	1	Backstitch
	Roof and chimney	Gray	6	Backstitch
	Door	Brown	6	Backstitch
	Path	Golden yellow	3	Running Stitch*
Outline and fill	Snow	Light aqua	6	French Knot
	Treetop	Dark green	6	Backstitch
	Tree trunk	Brown	6	Backstitch
Embroider	Tree decorations	Turquoise / Pale pink	6/6	(Tiny) Straight Stitches
	Doorknob	Dark brown	3	French Knot

* Use alternating long and short stitches.

Jolly Snowman

Embroidery pattern is on page 141.

EMBROIDERY FLOSS: pale pink, golden yellow, red, aqua, dark brown, gray, orange, pale green

Jolly Snowman Embroidery Guide

	Element	Color	# of strands	Stitches
Double outline	Head and body	Pale pink	6	Backstitch
Outline	Hat	Golden yellow	6	Backstitch
	Scarf stripes	Red/Aqua	6/6	Backstitch
	Snowballs	Pale pink	3	Split Stitch
	Mouth	Dark brown	1	French Knot
Outline and fill	Hat ribbon	Gray	3	Backstitch
	Nose	Orange	6	Backstitch
	Holly leaf	Pale green	2	Backstitch
Embroider	Scarf tassels	Aqua	6	French Knot and Straight Stitch
	Eyes	Dark brown	3	French Knot
	Buttons	Dark brown	6	French Knot
	Holly berries	Red	6	French Knot

Little Robin

Embroidery pattern is on page 137.

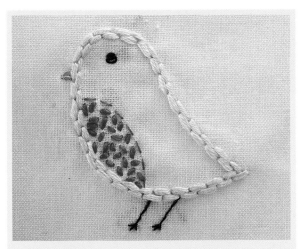

EMBROIDERY FLOSS: pale pink, red, dark brown, aqua

Little Robin Embroidery Guide

	Element	Color	# of strands	Stitch
Double outline	Head and body	Pale pink	6	Backstitch
Outline	Breast	Red	1	Running Stitch
	Legs and feet	Dark brown	1	Backstitch
	Beak	Aqua	2	Backstitch
	Eye	Dark brown	1	Backstitch and French Knot
Fill	Breast	Red	6	Seed Stitch

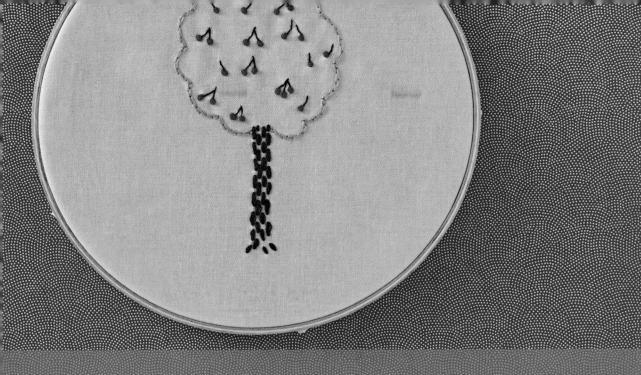

EVERYDAY PRETTINESS

Lemonade Coaster • Rain, Rain, Go Away Hanging Hoop • Lost in Stitch Tissue Box Cover
"Oh, My Balloon!" Hot Water Bottle Cover

Life goes on. The daily repetitive grind can sometimes seem
mundane, but there can be something equally soothing in the
gentle rhythms of the everyday. Add a little cuteness here and
there to turn the daily "expected" into a bit of daily comfort.

Finished size: 4″ × 4″ (10cm × 10cm) • *Designed and made by Aneela Hoey*

Lemonade Coaster

One of my favorite childhood memories is of being allowed to add a shake of salt to a glass of fizzy lemonade or lemon soda. It makes the drink fizz up into a mass of white froth that can easily spill over the top of the glass if you don't drink it super fast!

Because the embroidery and sewing in this project are simple, it is an ideal starter project. Why not make a set of coasters, each embroidered with a different motif?

MATERIALS

- 8″ × 8″ (20cm × 20cm) piece of white cotton fabric • 5″ × 5″ (13cm × 13cm) piece of batting
- 5″ × 5″ (13cm × 13cm) piece of print fabric for the backing • 2½″ × 26″ (6.5cm × 66cm) strip of print fabric for the binding • 5″ (13cm) embroidery hoop

EMBROIDERY FLOSS: aqua, pale yellow

Embroidery

Embroidery pattern is on page 143.

Transfer the pattern onto the center of the 8″ × 8″ white fabric and fix it in the hoop, as described in Embroidery Basics (page 8). Refer to the embroidery guide to embroider the design.

Lemonade Embroidery Guide

	Element	Color	# of strands	Stitch
Outline and fill	Lemonade	Pale yellow	4	Running Stitch
Outline	Jug / Glass	Aqua	2	Backstitch
	Jug pattern	Aqua	1	Backstitch

*For three more embroidery
designs, see Alternate Embroidery
Patterns (pages 101–103).*

Coaster

1. Remove the embroidery from the hoop and press with an iron, as described in Ironing (page 32), taking care not to iron the embroidered parts.

2. Cut the embroidered fabric down to 5˝ × 5˝, keeping the embroidery centered.

3. Place the backing fabric wrong side up; top it with the batting and then with the embroidered square, right side up.

4. Refer to Quiltmaking Techniques (page 131) to machine quilt the piece with a 1˝ grid pattern.

5. Trim the coaster to 4˝ × 4˝, keeping the embroidery centered.

6. Make and sew on the binding as described in Binding (page 133).

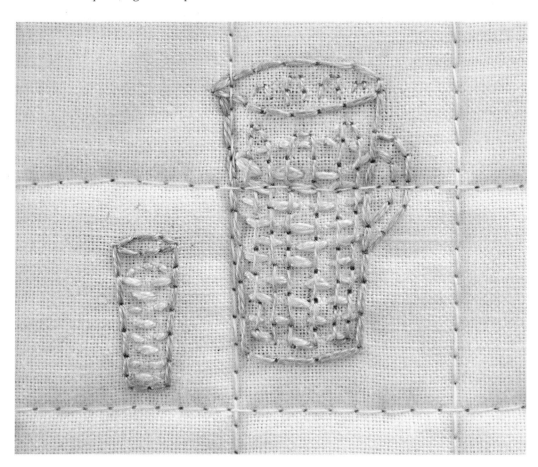

Alternate Embroidery Patterns

Transfer your chosen pattern onto the center of the 8″ × 8″ white fabric and fix it in the hoop, as described in Embroidery Basics (page 8). Embroider according to the embroidery guide for each pattern. When the embroidery is finished, follow the instructions for Coaster (page 100).

Cherry

Embroidery pattern is on page 143.

EMBROIDERY FLOSS: gray, red, aqua

Cherry Embroidery Guide

	Element	Color	# of strands	Stitch
Outline	Stem	Gray	6	Backstitch
	Cherries	Red	1	Running Stitch
	Leaves	Aqua	4	Backstitch*
	Leaf veins	Aqua	1	Backstitch
Fill	Cherries	Red	6	Seed Stitch

* Use alternating long and short stitches.

Leaves

Embroidery pattern is on page 143.

EMBROIDERY FLOSS: medium green, pale green, brown, red, aqua

Leaves Embroidery Guide

	Element	Color	# of strands	Stitch
Double outline	Medium green leaf	Medium green	6	Backstitch
	Medium green leaf veins	Medium green	1	Running Stitch
	Pale green leaf	Pale green / Medium green	6/1	Couching Stitch
	Pale green leaf veins	Pale green	6	Backstitch
Outline	Brown leaf	Brown	5	Backstitch*
	Brown leaf veins	Brown	1	Backstitch
	Red leaf	Red	2	Running Stitch
	Red leaf veins	Red	4	Split Stitch
	Aqua leaf	Aqua	6	Split Stitch
	Aqua leaf veins	Aqua	2	Running Stitch

* Use alternating long and short stitches.

Popsicle

Embroidery pattern is on page 143.

EMBROIDERY FLOSS: brown, pale pink, orange, beige, deep pink, yellow, pink, blue, medium pink

Popsicle Embroidery Guide

	Element	Color	# of strands	Stitches
Outline	Popsicle tip	Brown	6	Backstitch
	Pale pink stripe	Pale pink	6	Backstitch
	Orange stripe	Orange	6	Backstitch
	Stick	Beige	1	Backstitch
	Bottom edge of popsicle	Orange	3	Running Stitch
Outline and fill	Deep pink stripe	Deep pink	6	Backstitch
	Yellow stripe	Yellow	6	Backstitch
Fill	Pale pink stripe	Pale pink	6	Running Stitch
	Orange stripe	Orange	6	Running Stitch
Embroider	Sprinkles	Pink / Blue / Medium pink / Yellow / Orange	3 of each	Seed Stitch

Finished size: 7″ (18cm) in diameter • *Designed and made by Aneela Hoey*

Rain, Rain, Go Away Hanging Hoop

When the rain is falling down outside, stay indoors and stitch up this pretty piece instead of going out! This is a great way to stitch and then display an embroidery, right in its hoop.

Embroidery

Embroidery pattern is on page 144.

Transfer the pattern, with the figure slightly right of center on the 12″ × 12″ fabric, and fix it in the hoop, as described in Embroidery Basics (page 8). Refer to the embroidery guide to embroider the design.

For three more embroidery designs, see Alternate Embroidery Patterns (pages 107–109).

Rain, Rain Go Away Embroidery Guide

	Element	Color	# of strands	Stitch
	Umbrella	Medium bright pink / Pale pink	6/1	Couching Stitch
Outline	Center panel of umbrella	Medium deep pink	6	Backstitch
	Face / Nose / Hand / Legs	Beige	1	Backstitch
	Umbrella handle	Gray	6	Backstitch
Outline and fill	Sweater	Red	6	Backstitch
	Skirt	Burgundy	6	Backstitch
	Boots	Medium bright pink	3	Backstitch
	Hair	Golden yellow	3	Backstitch
Embroider	Umbrella tips	Medium pink	6	French Knot
	Eye	Dark brown	1	Straight Stitch
	Mouth	Red	1	Backstitch
	Rain	Pale pink	6	Straight Stitch

Hanging Hoop

1. Make sure that the fabric is still taut and flat in the embroidery hoop. Pull the excess fabric outside of the hoop gently on all sides to remove any slack made during stitching.

2. Use a screwdriver to tighten the hoop screw top as much as possible.

3. With a pencil, draw a line all around the excess fabric, ½″ away from the outside of the hoop. Use pinking shears to cut on this line.

4. Turn the hoop over, wrong side up. Dab a tiny amount of fabric glue along the inside of the inner hoop. Turn the pinked fabric edge and press it onto the glue for a few seconds to secure it to the back of the hoop. Continue to glue all around the inner hoop edge, working about an inch at a time (see below).

5. Set aside for several hours until completely dry.

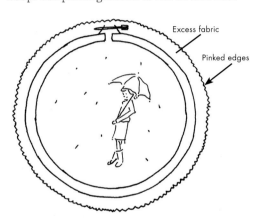

Excess fabric

Pinked edges

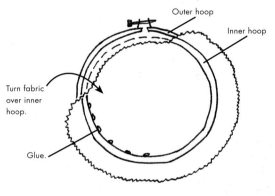

Outer hoop

Inner hoop

Turn fabric over inner hoop.

Glue.

Alternate Embroidery Patterns

Transfer your chosen pattern onto the center of the 12″ × 12″ fabric and fix it in the hoop, as described in Embroidery Basics (page 8). Embroider according to the embroidery guide for each pattern. When the embroidery is finished, follow the instructions for Hanging Hoop (above).

Quack, Quack Duck

Embroidery pattern is on page 138.

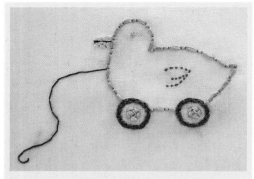

EMBROIDERY FLOSS: golden yellow, red, brown, pale pink, beige, dark brown, aqua

Quack, Quack Duck Embroidery Guide

	Element	Color	# of strands	Stitch
Outline	Duck	Golden yellow	6	Backstitch*
	Wing	Red	2	(Tiny) Running Stitch
	String	Brown	1	Backstitch
Double outline	Wheels	Brown	4	Backstitch
Outline and fill	Beak	Pale pink	4	Backstitch
	Wheel center	Beige	6	Backstitch
Embroider	Beak center	Dark brown	1	Backstitch
	Eye	Aqua	2	French Knot

* Use alternating long and short stitches.

Race Car

Embroidery pattern is on page 138.

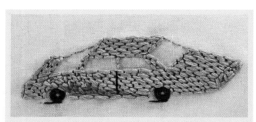

EMBROIDERY FLOSS: golden yellow, gray, aqua, brown, orange, dark brown

Race Car Embroidery Guide

	Element	Color	# of strands	Stitch
Outline	Flame detail on car	Golden yellow	6	Backstitch
	Front and rear windows	Gray	1	Running Stitch
	Door edge	Dark brown	1	Backstitch
Outline and fill	Car	Aqua	6	Backstitch
	Wheels	Brown	3	Backstitch
Fill	Head lights	Golden yellow	2	Backstitch
	Flame detail on car	Orange	6	Backstitch
Embroider	Shadow (under wheels)	Dark brown	1	Backstitch
	Speed marks	Dark brown	1	Straight Stitch

Singing Cherry Tree

Embroidery pattern is on page 145.

EMBROIDERY FLOSS: pale green, brown, dark brown, red

Singing Cherry Tree Embroidery Guide

	Element	Color	# of strands	Stitch
Double outline	Treetop	Pale green	3	Backstitch
Outline and fill	Tree trunk	Brown	6	Running Stitch
Embroider	Cherry stems	Dark brown	1	Backstitch
	Cherries	Red	6	French Knot

Finished size: to fit box, 9¼″ long × 4½″ wide × 3″ tall (23.5cm long × 11.4cm wide × 7.6cm tall)

Designed and made by Aneela Hoey

Lost in Stitch Tissue Box Cover

Feeling a little under the weather? This pretty little tissue box cover is sure to brighten up the gloomiest of colds, and it makes a charming little cover-up for garish-looking packaging. The cover can be embroidered on either one or both sides of the tissue slot; this version is embroidered on both.

MATERIALS

- ⅝ yard (0.6m) of white cotton fabric • ½ yard (0.5m) of ¼″ (6mm)-wide elastic
- 5″ (13cm) embroidery hoop • Tapestry needle

EMBROIDERY FLOSS: beige, dark brown, medium brown, pink, light beige, gray, red, bright turquoise, light aqua, light pink, golden yellow, orange

---

TIP

Tissue box sizes can vary; if yours differs from the one shown, measure and make slight adjustments to the sizes of the cover pieces to ensure a perfect fit.

CUTTING

White fabric:

Cut 1 piece 5¾″ × 29″ for the sides.

Cut 1 piece 10″ × 15″ for the decorative flap.

Cut 1 piece 5″ × 9¾″ for the cover top.

Embroidery

Embroidery patterns are on pages 139 and 144.

1. On the decorative flap piece, use a pencil to draw a ½″-wide border all the way around the edge.

2. Fold the decorative flap piece in half along the length; gently make a crease with the palm of your hand, and then open out the piece and turn it right side up.

3. Place the *Lost in Stitch* embroidery pattern inside the drawn border, centered below the crease, making sure the top of the girl's head is placed at least ½″ below the crease and her feet are placed at least 1″ above the drawn border along the lower edge. Refer to the photograph of the finished embroidery for placement. Transfer the *Lost in Stitch* embroidery pattern onto the flap, as described in Embroidery Basics (page 8).

For three more embroidery designs, see Alternate Embroidery Patterns (pages 117–119).

LOST IN STITCH TISSUE BOX COVER

Optional: Place the *Bird in a Hoop* embroidery pattern on the other half of the decorative flap, centered below the crease, making sure the top of the image is placed at least ½″ below the crease and the bottom of the image is at least ¾″ above the drawn border along the lower edge. Refer to the photo (at left). Transfer the *Bird in a Hoop* embroidery pattern onto the flap, as described in Embroidery Basics (page 8).

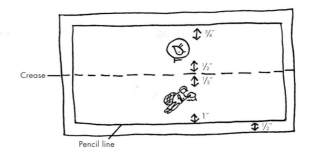

Crease

Pencil line

LOST IN STITCH
EMBROIDERY

Fix the fabric half with the *Lost in Stitch* pattern in the embroidery hoop and tighten as described in Embroidery Basics (page 8). Refer to the embroidery guide to embroider the design.

Lost in Stitch Embroidery Guide

	Element	Color	# of strands	Stitch
Outline	Face / Neck / Hands / Arm	Beige	1	Backstitch
	Embroidery fabric	Dark brown	1	Backstitch
Outline and fill	Hair	Medium brown	3	Backstitch
	T-shirt	Pink	6	Split stitch
	Collar	Light beige	3	Backstitch
	Jeans	Gray	6	Backstitch
	Hexagon patches on cushion	Red / Bright turquoise / Light aqua / Light pink / Golden yellow / Orange	4 of each	Split Stitch*
	Reverse of cushion	Light aqua	6	Backstitch
	Sock stripes	Light pink / Light aqua	3/3	Backstitch
Embroider	Eyes	Dark brown	1	Straight Stitch
	Nose	Beige	1	Straight Stitch
	Mouth	Red	1	Straight Stitch
	Embroidery	Red	1	Cross-Stitch

* Fill with stitches going clockwise in each patch.

OPTIONAL:
BIRD IN A HOOP
EMBROIDERY

Remove the embroidered fabric from the hoop. Rehoop, fixing the fabric half with the *Bird in a Hoop* pattern in the embroidery hoop; tighten. Refer to the embroidery guide to embroider the design.

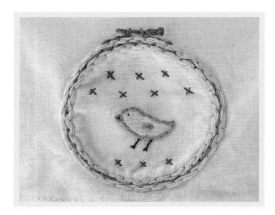

Bird in a Hoop Embroidery Guide

	Element	Color	# of strands	Stitch
Outline and fill	Hoop	Light beige	6	Backstitch
	Screw holder and screw	Beige	2	Backstitch
Outline	Center line on hoop	Gray	2	Backstitch
	Bird/Wing	Golden yellow	2	Split Stitch
Embroider	Crosses	Red	1	Cross-Stitch
	Beak	Beige	2	Backstitch
	Legs	Dark brown	1	Backstitch
	Eye	Dark brown	1	(Tiny) Straight Stitch
	Line on beak	Dark brown	1	Straight Stitch

Tissue Box Cover

All seam allowances are ¼″ unless otherwise noted.

First prepare the embroidered decorative flap and then stitch it onto the tissue box cover's plain top and sides.

DECORATIVE FLAP

1. Remove the embroidery from the hoop and press with an iron, as described in Ironing (page 32), taking care not to iron the embroidered parts. Using a rotary cutter, cutting mat, and ruler, cut along the pencil lines marking the border.

2. Fold over the edges of the decorative flap ¼″ to the wrong side and press.

3. With the fabric still wrong side up, make a light pencil mark 1″ away from each corner on both folded edges. (Figure A)

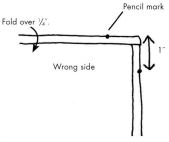

Figure A

4. Use the pencil marks to fold the corners diagonally to the wrong side and press. Trim across the folded corner ¼″ from the fold. (Figure B)

5. Fold over each side edge ½″ to the wrong side; press to make a mitered corner. (Figure C)

6. Turn right side up and machine stitch all around the decorative flap ⅜″ from the outside folded edges.

7. For the tissue box cover "slot," draw a line along the center crease with a pencil, starting 3½″ from each short edge. Set the decorative flap aside. (Figure D)

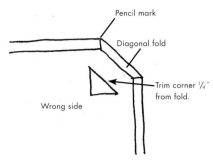

Figure B

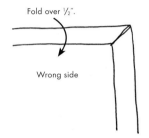

Figure C

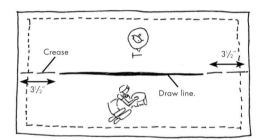

Figure D

COVER ASSEMBLY

1. Fold the cover top piece in half along the length and gently make a crease with the palm of your hand. Open out the piece and turn it right side up. Draw a pencil line along the crease line, starting 2″ from each short edge.

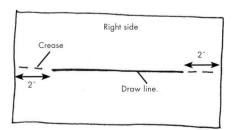

2. Place the cover top piece underneath the side strip, right sides together and with the long edges aligned along the top edge. Arrange the pieces so that the short edge of the side strip extends ¼″ to the left of the short edge of the top piece.

3. Beginning ½″ from the short edge of the side strip, machine stitch down the first long edge, stopping ¼″ before the second short edge of the top piece, with the needle in the down position.

4. Keeping the needle in the down position, raise the presser foot and pivot the unstitched part of the side strip 90° to align it neatly with the next short edge of the cover top piece below.

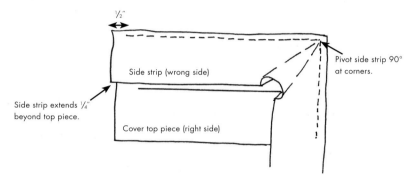

½″

Side strip (wrong side)

Pivot side strip 90° at corners.

Side strip extends ¼″ beyond top piece.

Cover top piece (right side)

5. Stitch the remaining edges together, pivoting at each of the next 2 corners, as described in Steps 3 and 4. Stitch back to the beginning corner.

6. Remove the piece from the machine. Align the short edges of the side strip at the beginning corner. Pin and stitch them together with a ¼″ seam allowance. Trim any excess fabric.

7. Refer to Seam Finishes (page 59) to zigzag or overlock the raw edges to finish them. Reinforce the corners with a little extra stitching for durability.

8. Place the flap onto the top piece, *right sides facing up.* Match up the pencil lines; pin. Hand baste all around, ½″ away from the pencil lines. Carefully cut along the pencil lines through both layers. Zigzag or overlock stitch all around the cut line. Remove the basting.

9. To make a casing for the elastic, fold over the side raw edge ¼″ to the wrong side and press. Fold it over another ½″ and press again. Leaving a 1″ opening along one short end, stitch all around the casing ⅜″ from the outer folded edge.

10. Thread the elastic onto a tapestry needle. From the opening, insert the needle into the casing, pulling the elastic through and back out of the opening. Pin the ends of the elastic together with a safety pin.

11. Carefully fit the cover over the tissue box and tighten the elastic so that the cover stays in place. Overlap the elastic ends and repin them. Remove the cover from the box and zigzag stitch the elastic ends together securely. Trim the excess elastic down to 1″ on either side of the stitching. Insert the ends into the casing and hand sew the opening closed, as described in Finishing the Binding (page 135).

Alternate Embroidery Patterns

The tissue box cover can be embroidered on one or both sides of the tissue slot. If you wish to embroider two patterns, pick a second pattern of your choice from these pages or from the patterns at the back of the book. Make sure the height of the pattern is no more than 2¾″.

Follow the steps for *Lost in Stitch Tissue Box Cover* (page 110) to position your chosen embroidery pattern. Transfer the pattern and fix it in the hoop, as described in Embroidery Basics (page 8). Embroider according to the embroidery guide for each pattern. When the embroidery is finished, follow the remaining instructions for Tissue Box Cover (page 114).

An Apple a Day

Embroidery pattern is on page 140.

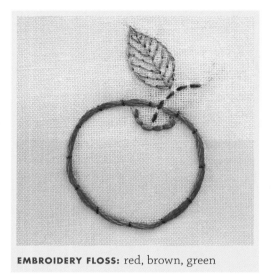

EMBROIDERY FLOSS: red, brown, green

An Apple a Day Embroidery Guide

	Element	Color	# of strands	Stitch
Outline	Apple	Red/Brown	6/1	Couching Stitch
	Leaf / Leaf veins	Green	1	Backstitch
Embroider	Stem	Brown	3	Running Stitch
	Dimple at top of apple	Red	6	Backstitch

Lily of the Valley

Embroidery pattern is on page 145.

EMBROIDERY FLOSS: pale green, medium green, dark green, pale pink

Lily of the Valley Embroidery Guide

	Element	Color	# of strands	Stitch
Outline	Leaves	Pale green	6	Backstitch
Embroider	Leaf veins	Medium green	3	Split Stitch
	Stems	Dark green	1	Backstitch
	Flowers	Pale pink	6	French Knot

Pull-along Train

Embroidery pattern is on page 145.

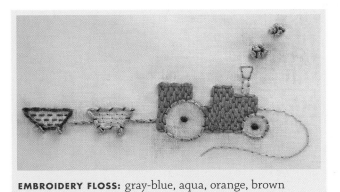

EMBROIDERY FLOSS: gray-blue, aqua, orange, brown

Pull-along Train Embroidery Guide

	Element	Color	# of strands	Stitch
Outline	Engine wheels	Gray-blue	6	Backstitch
	Funnel tube	Aqua	3	Backstitch
	Funnel	Orange	1	Backstitch
	First cart	Aqua/ Brown	6/1	Couching Stitch
	Second cart	Brown	6	Backstitch
Outline and fill	Engine	Orange	6	Backstitch
Fill	Smoke	Gray-blue	6	French Knot
Embroider	Pull-along string	Gray-blue	1	Backstitch
	Lines on first cart	Aqua	1	Backstitch
	Lines on second cart	Brown	1	Running Stitch
	Engine wheels center	Brown	6	French Knot
	Cart wheels	Gray-blue	6	French Knot
	Links	Gray-blue	3	Split Stitch

Finished size: 9½″ × 15½″ (24.1cm × 39.4cm) • *Designed and made by Aneela Hoey*

"Oh, My Balloon" Hot Water Bottle Cover

If it's chilly outside or you are feeling under the weather, use this cute quilted cover to house a hot water bottle to help you stay warm and dreamy on a cloudy day (balloons lost or otherwise).

MATERIALS

• 1 yard (0.9m) of white cotton fabric • ½ yard (0.5m) of cotton fabric for the lining • ¼ yard (0.25m) of print fabric for the binding • 18″ × 40″ (46cm × 102cm) piece of batting • 2 pieces of thin cardboard, each approximately 11″ × 17″ (28cm × 43cm) (Tape pieces together, as needed, to make templates.) • 7″ (18cm) embroidery hoop

EMBROIDERY FLOSS: beige, red, light pink, light aqua, golden yellow, dark brown, orange

CUTTING

White fabric:

Cut 1 piece 14″ × 20″ for the cover back.

Cut 1 piece 14″ × 15″ for the cover front.

Cut 1 piece 14″ × 12″ for the cover flap.

Hot Water Bottle Cover Pattern

1. Enlarge and copy the *Hot Water Bottle Cover* template pattern (page 127). Cut out the paper pattern. With a pencil, trace around the outside edge onto the thin cardboard to make the back template.

Fold the paper pattern down along the front tracing line to make the front pattern. Trace along the foldline and around the outside edge below the foldline onto the thin cardboard to make the front template.

Open out the paper pattern and cut it along the flap tracing line to make the flap pattern. Trace the flap pattern onto the thin cardboard to make the flap template.

Cut out all three cardboard templates.

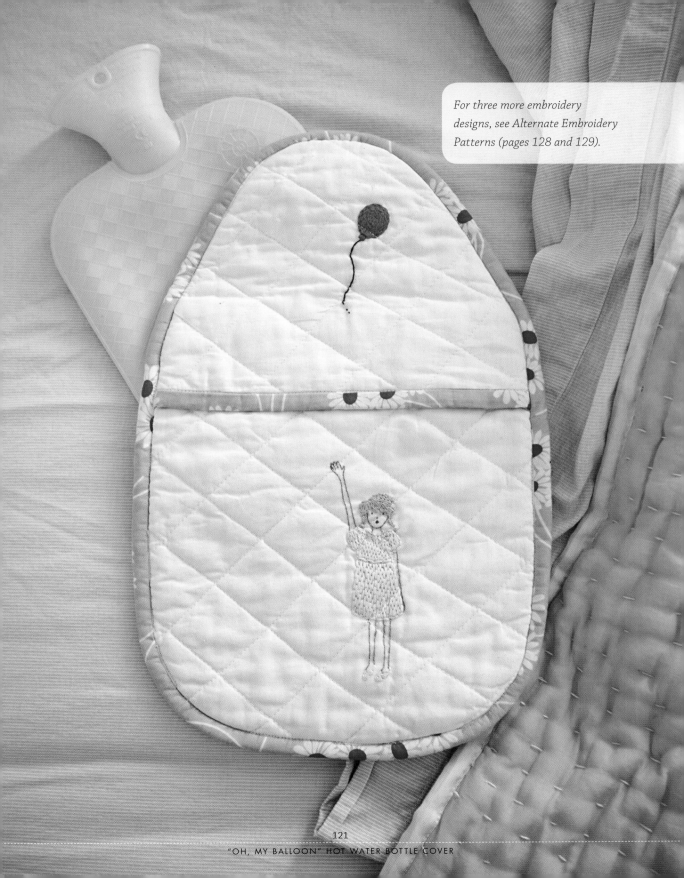

For three more embroidery designs, see Alternate Embroidery Patterns (pages 128 and 129).

2. Use the flap template and a pencil to draw the shape onto the 14″ wide × 12″ high white cotton fabric, the lining fabric, and the batting. Do not cut out the pieces yet.

Use the front template to draw the shape onto the 14″ wide × 15″ high white cotton fabric, the lining fabric, and the batting. Do not cut out the pieces yet.

Use the back template to draw the shape onto the 14″ wide × 20″ high piece of white cotton fabric, the lining fabric, and the batting. Do not cut out the pieces yet.

Embroidery

Embroidery patterns are on page 146.

GIRL IN A PINK DRESS EMBROIDERY

1. Place the *Girl in a Pink Dress* embroidery pattern onto the bottom half of the white front piece, inside the drawn shape, slightly off-center, and at least 1″ away from the lower edge. Refer to the finished embroidery project photo (page 121) for placement.

2. Transfer the pattern to the fabric and fix it in the hoop, as described in Embroidery Basics (page 8). Refer to the embroidery guide to embroider the design. Remove the fabric from the hoop when finished embroidering.

Girl in a Pink Dress Embroidery Guide

	Element	Color	# of strands	Stitch
Outline	Face / Neck / Arms / Hands / Legs	Beige	1	Backstitch
	Lips	Red	1	Backstitch
	Collar	Light aqua	3	Backstitch
Outline and fill	Dress	Light pink	6	Backstitch
	Hair (except braids)	Golden yellow	4	Backstitch
	Shoes	Light pink	3	Backstitch
Fill	Collar	Light aqua	3	Satin Stitch
Embroider	Waistband	Light aqua	3	Backstitch
	Hair braids	Golden yellow	4	Straight Stitch
	Eyes	Dark brown	1	Straight Stitch
	Nose	Beige	1	Straight Stitch

123

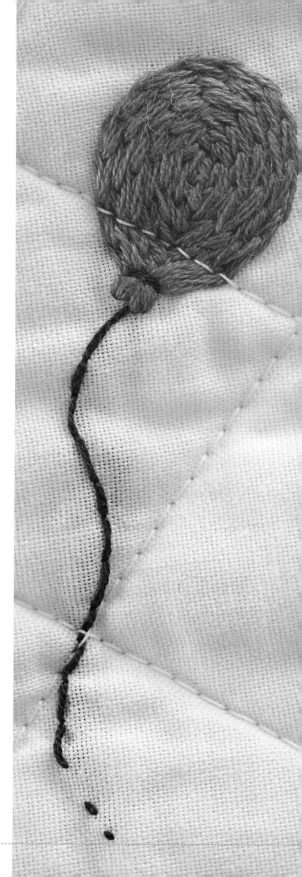

BALLOON EMBROIDERY

1. Place the *Balloon* embroidery pattern onto the white flap piece, inside the drawn shape, slightly off center, and at least 2″ away from each of the drawn edges. Refer to the finished embroidery project photo (page 121) for placement.

2. Transfer the pattern to the fabric and fix it in the hoop, as described in Embroidery Basics (page 8). Refer to the embroidery guide to embroider the design. Remove the fabric from the hoop when finished embroidering.

Balloon Embroidery Guide

	Element	Color	# of strands	Stitch
Outline and fill	Balloon	Orange	6	Backstitch
Embroider	String	Dark brown	2	Backstitch and Running Stitch

Hot Water Bottle Cover

All seam allowances are ¼″ unless otherwise noted.

QUILTING

1. Press the embroideries with an iron, as described in Ironing (page 32), taking care not to iron the embroidered parts.

2. Cut out the cover front and flap from the embroidered fabrics along the drawn lines. Cut out all the remaining flap, front, and back pieces along the drawn lines.

3. Layer the pattern pieces as follows: Place the flap lining piece wrong side up, lay the flap batting piece on top, and then place the embroidered flap on top of that, right side up. Make sure the edges of all 3 layers are aligned; pin. Layer the front and back pieces in the same way.

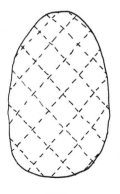

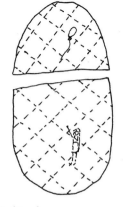

Quilting diagram

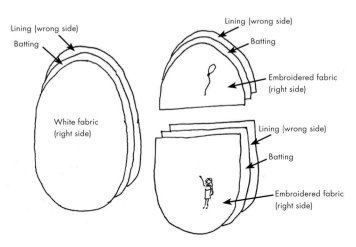

4. Set up your sewing machine with a walking foot for quilting. Using a creasing tool and a ruler, mark diagonal lines 1½″ apart in both directions on each of the 3 sandwiched pattern parts, as shown in the quilting diagram (top right).

5. Quilt along the creased lines, removing the pins as you go and backstitching at the beginning and end of each stitching line. Refer to Quiltmaking Techniques (page 131).

ASSEMBLY

1. Cut the binding fabric into 3 strips 2½″ wide × 40″ long. Refer to Binding (page 133) to join and fold the strips to make one long strip.

2. From the binding, cut off 2 strips, each measuring 10½″ in length.

3. Pin one of the strips along the straight edge of the quilted flap, aligning the raw edges.

4. Pin the second binding strip to the straight edge of the quilted front, aligning the raw edges.

5. Machine stitch the bindings in place. Trim away the excess binding; fold over and hand sew the folded edges in place on the back as described in Binding (page 133).

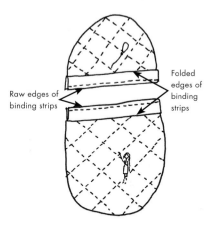

Raw edges of binding strips

Folded edges of binding strips

6. Place the quilted back on a flat surface, lining side up. Top with the quilt front, embroidered side up, aligning the side and bottom edges.

7. Position the flap on top, embroidered side up, aligning the top and side edges with the back. Pin and hand baste all the pieces together.

8. Beginning at the center bottom edge, machine stitch the binding in place all around the outside edge, using a ¼″ seam allowance.

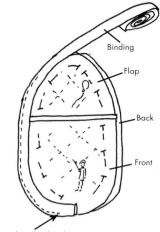

Binding

Flap

Back

Front

Start stitching binding here.

TIP

For extra reinforcement, stitch a few extra stitches or a machine-stitched bar tack in the binding seam allowance on either side of the flap opening before hand sewing the binding to the cover back. Consult your sewing machine manual for bar tack settings.

9. Fold over and hand sew the binding to the cover back.

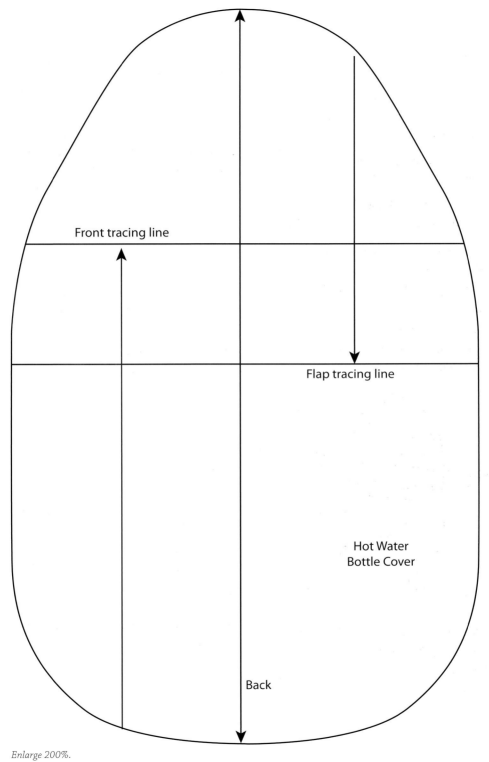

Front tracing line

Flap tracing line

Hot Water
Bottle Cover

Back

Enlarge 200%.

"OH, MY BALLOON" HOT WATER BOTTLE COVER

Alternate Embroidery Patterns

Follow the *"Oh, My Balloon" Hot Water Bottle Cover* pattern instructions (page 120) to prepare the front, back, and flap pieces. Transfer your chosen pattern onto the center of the bottom half of the white front piece, at least 1˝–2˝ from the bottom drawn line. Fix it in the hoop, as described in Embroidery Basics (page 8), and embroider according to the embroidery guide for each pattern. When the embroidery is finished, follow the instructions for Hot Water Bottle Cover (page 125).

For the alternative pattern options, leave the flap part of the cover unembroidered.

Little Deer

Embroidery pattern is on page 145.

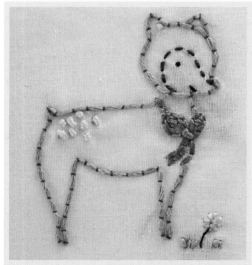

EMBROIDERY FLOSS: golden yellow, brown, pale pink, medium pink, dark brown, aqua, light aqua, dark green

Little Deer Embroidery Guide

	Element	Color	# of strands	Stitch
Outline	Head and body	Golden yellow / Brown	6/1	Couching Stitch
	Patch on face	Brown	3	Running Stitch
	Inner ear	Pale pink	6	Backstitch
Outline and fill	Ribbon	Medium pink	6	Backstitch
Embroider	Ribbon knot	Medium pink	6	French Knot
	Spots on back	Pale pink	6	French Knot
	Eye	Dark brown	2	French Knot
	Mouth	Dark brown	2	Straight Stitch
	Nose	Aqua	6	French Knot
	Flower center	Aqua	2	French Knot
	Petals	Light aqua	2	Straight Stitch
	Stem	Dark green	1	Backstitch
	Grass	Aqua	6	Straight Stitch

A Sweet Fox

Embroidery pattern is on page 144.

EMBROIDERY FLOSS: gray, brown, orange, dark brown

A Sweet Fox Embroidery Guide

	Element	Color	# of strands	Stitch
Outline	Tail tip	Gray	2	Running Stitch
	Nose	Brown	1	Backstitch
Outline and fill	Head and body	Orange	6	Split Stitch
Embroider	Eyes	Dark brown	2	French Knot
	Nose tip	Brown	6	Straight Stitch
	Mouth	Dark brown	2	Backstitch
	Toes	Gray	1	Straight Stitch

Notions

Embroidery pattern is on page 144.

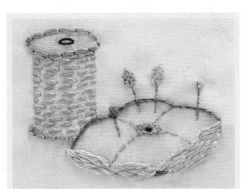

EMBROIDERY FLOSS: green, yellow, golden yellow, dark brown, light aqua, light pink, aqua, pale green, turquoise, pink, orange, gray

Notions Embroidery Guide

	Element	Color	# of strands	Stitch
Outline	Top edge of pincushion	Green	6	Split Stitch
	Top and bottom of thread spool	Golden yellow	6	Backstitch
	Center of spool top	Dark brown	1	Backstitch
Double outline	Button on pincushion	Yellow	3	Backstitch
Outline and fill	Sides of pincushion	Light aqua/ Light pink	6/1	Couching Stitch
	Oval pin tops	Aqua/ Yellow	3/3	Backstitch
Fill	Thread on spool	Pale green	6	Running Stitch
Embroider	Shadow (under pincushion)	Green	3	Straight Stitch
	Stitched lines on pincushion	Turquoise	1	Running Stitch
	Stitched cross on button	Dark brown	1	Cross-Stitch
	Round pin tops	Pink/Orange	6/6	French Knot
	Pins	Gray	1	Backstitch

"OH, MY BALLOON" HOT WATER BOTTLE COVER

QUILTMAKING TECHNIQUES

For some of the projects in this book, you will need to use basic quiltmaking techniques. In this section, I outline my methods; if you have your own preferred methods, by all means use them. This is not meant to be a complete quiltmaking primer. If you are a beginner, consult some of the many books available, including *The Practical Guide to Patchwork* by Elizabeth Hartman (available from C&T Publishing). Several tools and supplies are mentioned in this section; for more information on these, refer to Sewing Tool Kit (page 34).

Making a Quilt Sandwich

Before quilting a quilt or other piece, you must layer and baste the quilt top, batting, and backing. The method is the same as for a quilt, such as *Let's Go Fly a Kite Baby Quilt* (page 78), or a smaller item, such as *Lemonade Coaster* (page 98)—except that with smaller items, you can work on a table instead of the floor.

1. Press the backing fabric and place it wrong side up on a clean floor. Using masking tape, tape down the edges at intervals, taking care to keep the fabric taut but not stretched.

2. Center the batting on the backing fabric. The batting and backing should be at least 2″ larger than the quilt top all around (or up to 1″ larger all around for smaller items). Beginning at the center, smooth everything out so that it is perfectly flat.

3. Press the embroidered fabric (quilt top), taking care not to iron the embroidered parts. Then center it right side up on the batting.

4. Beginning at the center and smoothing outward as you go, pin the 3 layers together at 2″–3″ intervals, using bent-arm quilting safety pins. Keep the layers as smooth and as flat as possible as you pin.

Quilting

Most of the quilted items in this book are quilted in either parallel lines or a grid format. I find this type of quilting really quick and easy to do, especially if you use a seam guide tool.

To quilt items with a sewing machine, you may wish to use a walking foot. If you are new to quilting, it is good idea to first make up a mini quilt sandwich, using two pieces of fabric about 10˝ × 10˝, with batting in between. Practice on that fabric, adjusting your machine's sewing tension if necessary and getting comfortable with the walking foot, until you get the hang of it.

QUILTING PARALLEL LINES

Using a creasing tool and a ruler, mark a straight, vertical line on your quilt sandwich. Fix the seam guide tool to your presser foot and set it at the width that you want between the rows of stitching. Place the curved foot of the tool onto the creased line and keep it on the marked line as you stitch the first row, removing pins as you go. Next, set the curved foot on the previously stitched line and create a second stitched line parallel to the first. Continue to stitch in parallel lines all across the quilt.

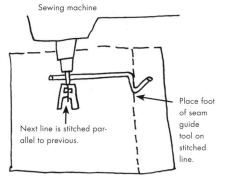

Sewing machine

Next line is stitched parallel to previous.

Place foot of seam guide tool on stitched line.

QUILTING A GRID

To quilt in a grid formation, first quilt vertically stitched lines as described in Quilting Parallel Lines. Next, mark the first horizontal line with the creasing tool and ruler, making sure this horizontal line is perpendicular to the vertical lines. Reset the distance between the presser foot and the curved foot of the seam guide tool, if instructed to do so in the project. Continue stitching as you did for the vertical lines.

When you have finished machine quilting, trim the quilt backing and batting down to the same size as the embroidered piece (quilt top), or as indicated in the project instructions.

Binding

I prefer to make and use double-fold binding to finish off quilted items.

MAKING THE BINDING

1. Cut the binding fabric into 2½″ strips along the length of the fabric.

2. With right sides facing, stitch the short ends of the strips together, using a ¼″ seam allowance, to make one long strip.

3. Press the seams open. Fold over a short end of the binding strip 1″ to the wrong side and press.

4. Fold the binding strip in half along the entire length, wrong sides together, pressing as you go.

Fold in half.

ATTACHING THE BINDING

1. Beginning midway along one side of the quilt top, align the raw edges of the folded binding strip with the raw edge of the quilt.

2. Pin all along the edge to the first corner, leaving the first 2″ of the binding unattached.

3. Machine stitch the binding to the first edge of the quilt, using a ¼″ seam allowance and stopping ¼″ away from the second edge at the first corner. (Remove the pins just before you reach them as you sew.) Take a couple of backstitches and then remove the quilt from machine.

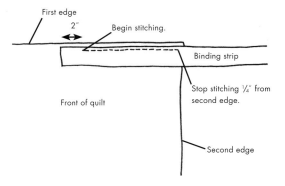

First edge

2″

Begin stitching.

Binding strip

Stop stitching ¼″ from second edge.

Front of quilt

Second edge

4. At the corner, fold the unattached part of the strip upward to make a 45° diagonal crease.

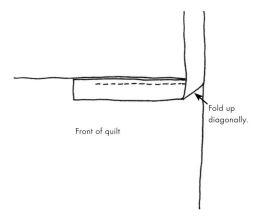

Fold up diagonally.

Front of quilt

5. Bring the binding strip down and align the raw edges with the second edge of the quilt, making a horizontal fold that's in line with the first quilt edge at the top right corner. This creates a nicely finished mitered corner.

6. Pin the strip to the second edge of the quilt up to the next corner. Begin stitching the strip to the edge, starting ¼˝ away from the first edge. (Backstitch at the beginning to secure the seam.) Stitch up to the next corner, stopping ¼˝ from the corner, removing the pins as you go, and continue as at the previous corner (see Steps 4 and 5).

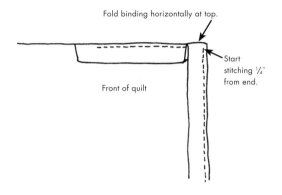

Fold binding horizontally at top.

Front of quilt

Start stitching ¼˝ from end.

7. Continue stitching each side and corner as in Step 6. On the fourth side, stop about 4˝ before reaching the starting point.

8. Overlap the 2 short ends of the binding by a couple of inches, and then cut off the excess binding.

9. Tuck the cut end of the binding neatly inside the folded end. Pin and continue stitching to secure it in place. Backstitch to finish it off.

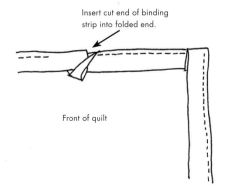

Insert cut end of binding strip into folded end.

Front of quilt

FINISHING THE BINDING

1. With the back of the quilt facing you, bring the folded edge of the binding over to the back and pin it in place all along the stitching line.

2. With a hand sewing needle and thread, make a few stitches hidden under the binding to secure the thread, stitching only through the backing and batting.

3. On the last of these first few stitches, bring the needle out through the binding, catching just a few threads close to the fold (exit point).

4. Insert the needle into the back of the quilt, through the backing and batting only, immediately under the exit point. Bring the needle back out through the fold of the binding as in Step 3, about ⅜˝ away.

5. Continue stitching all around the edge of the quilt. Secure with a few stitches to finish it off.

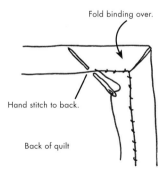

Fold binding over.

Hand stitch to back.

Back of quilt

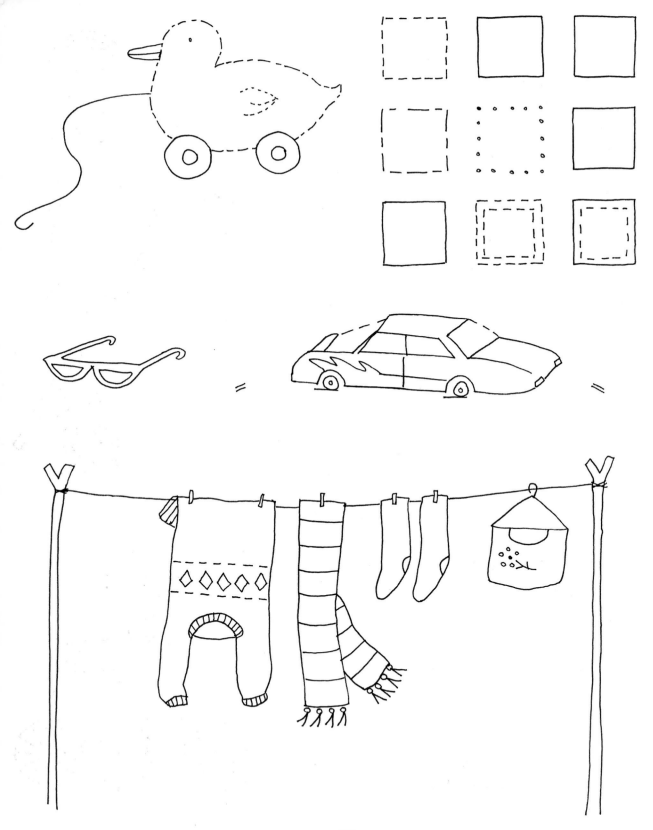

LITTLE STITCHES

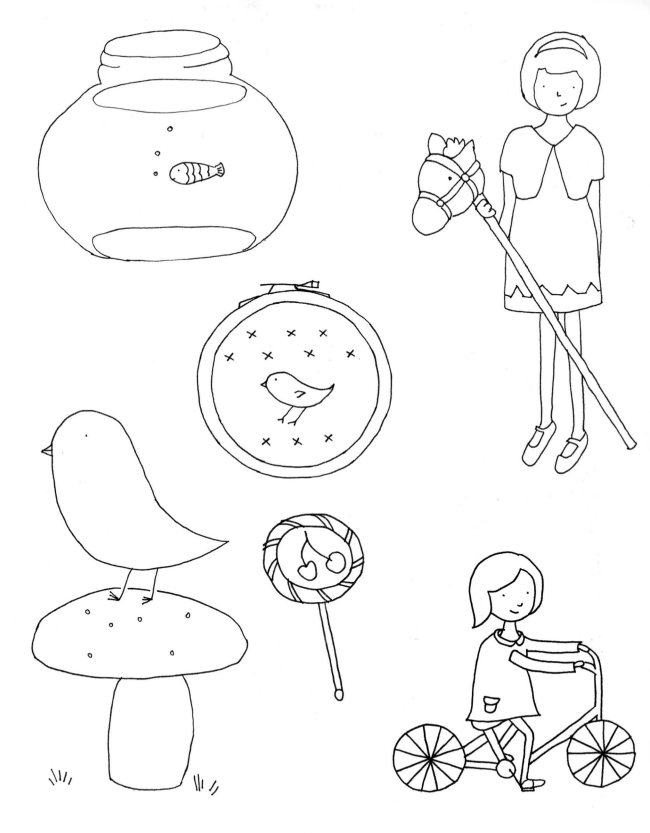

LITTLE STITCHES

LITTLE STITCHES

LITTLE STITCHES

LITTLE STITCHES

LITTLE STITCHES

About the Author

Aneela Hoey studied printed textile design at Winchester School of Art in the United Kingdom and went on to work at design studios in both London and New York. She now designs fabric lines for Moda Fabrics, as well as her own embroidery and quilt patterns, which she sells in her small online shop.

Aneela writes the popular blog ComfortStitching, where she catalogs her crafty endeavors and provides insights into her inspirations and design processes. She was also one of the founding members of the popular online e-zine *Fat Quarterly*.

Aneela lives in Berkshire, England, with her husband and two young daughters.

Photo by Asha Hoey

ANEELA'S SITES:

comfortstitching.typepad.co.uk
etsy.com/shop/comfortstitching

Online Resources

For embroidery flosses and notions:

purlsoho.com/purl
theworkroom.bigcartel.com